Erin Deering is an Australian entrepreneur. At the age of twenty-seven she co-founded Triangl, a global swimwear brand, and has been listed as one of Australia's top richest people under forty for six years in a row.

Since exiting the business in 2018, Erin is a sought-after keynote speaker and spends her time advising and mentoring other women on how to achieve balance while simultaneously chasing their dreams. Erin has appeared in *The Times, Bloomberg, The Independent, The Daily Telegraph, Vogue Australia,* and *The Sydney Morning Herald* as well as numerous publications and podcasts. She lives in Melbourne, with the love of her life, raising her four children.

Hanging by a Thread

ERIN DEERING

affirm press

affirm press

First published by Affirm Press in 2023
Boon Wurrung Country
28 Thistlethwaite Street
South Melbourne VIC 3205
affirmpress.com.au

10 9 8 7 6 5 4 3 2 1

 A catalogue record for this book is available from the National Library of Australia

ISBN: 9781922930194 (paperback)

Cover design by Josh Durham/Design by Committee © Affirm Press
Cover photograph by Darren McDonald
Back cover images: Marina Amelchugova, Chloe Latch, Michelle Alan
Typeset in Garamond Premier Pro 12/18 by J&M Typesetting
Proudly printed in Australia by McPherson's Printing Group

MIX
Paper | Supporting responsible forestry
FSC® C001695

For all my Triangl girls: my early adopters, my first influencers,
my Instagram followers, my one-time purchasers and my
loyal customers. It was always much more than just
a bikini to me.

I've come to realise something life-affirming from my
years before, during and now after Triangl. Simple, beautiful,
genuine connection with others (not some secret technique or formula!)
is how I truly define success in both my personal and professional life.

Thank you for letting me be a small part of your lives,
and I hope you enjoy the story of mine.

Contents

Prologue 1

Chapter One: Via the Shop Floor 5

Chapter Two: A Gap in the Market 21

Chapter Three: A Brand-new Life and a New Brand 33

Chapter Four: Lean, Keen Triangl Machine 55

Chapter Five: Taking Stock 73

Chapter Six: Triangl Girls 87

Chapter Seven: Scaling Up 101

Chapter Eight: My Oscar 115

Chapter Nine: Private Jets and Superyachts 137

Chapter Ten: Is This Freedom? 155

Chapter Eleven: Unravelling 167

Chapter Twelve: New Beginnings 185

Chapter Thirteen: Playing Pretend 193

Chapter Fourteen: Homecoming 203

Acknowledgements 223

Prologue

It was in Monaco in August 2016 that things really started to unravel. Despite living the high life jetsetting about the world, eating meals at the best restaurants, attending the coolest parties and going on frequent holidays – hell, we'd recently bought a new yacht – I was miserable. Craig and I were arguing over *everything*. And while our different points of view were what had helped us build our company, Triangl Swimwear, and make such a success of it – a business that was selling over 1000 swimsuits per day and had just been valued at over US$200 million – I was a mess. The money was rolling in so fast we hardly even noticed it anymore. Our son, Oscar, was only 16 months old, and I was badly sleep-deprived and basically starving myself. My eating disorder was raging out of control again along with my emotions, which were in a constant state of flux.

The sheer rage I felt at myself – for being this way, and for not being able to see my way out – pushed me over the edge.

Our new yacht was staffed by a very lovely crew of five, and a few were even my age (31), which was surreal in itself.

Craig and I were having yet another argument, which the crew were trying to ignore, I suppose, as they made themselves scarce. I stormed off the top deck where we had been screaming at each other – I can't even remember what that particular fight was about – and ran downstairs to our master bedroom. I looked out the windows at the deep blue of the Mediterranean Sea. We'd renovated the entire boat since we'd bought it, making the exterior matte black, and the interiors could have been featured in the pages of *Vogue Living*: neutral tones, cashmere blankets, a marble bathroom stocked with all the high-end amenities you could think of and custom lighting. It was a five-star hotel on water.

My designer 'resort wear' yacht wardrobe was hanging in the walk-in closet, meticulously unpacked on arrival by one of the crew.

I stormed through the room towards the bathroom, catching sight of myself in the mirror, wild-eyed.

I felt trapped. I clenched my fists, a rat in a cage. Pacing back and forth, I took small, frantic steps, trying to settle my thoughts and calm myself down. But it just wasn't possible. I was manic. I'd gone into my own world, my own private hell.

I grabbed my head with both hands, trying to squeeze out the chaotic thoughts, force them to slow down. But it didn't work. It never did. I sunk to the ground near the vanity and, with my left fist, started to punch myself repeatedly in the head, over and over again, feeling the lumps and bruises already rising. My conscious mind wasn't even engaged – I just wanted it all to stop. To be removed from the planet, to disappear.

The blinding headache that immediately followed calmed me somewhat – I was numb. That's what I was trying to achieve.

I started to cry. A quiet, almost gentle cry. I was so exhausted, and so sad.

I couldn't live like this anymore; I didn't want to live at all. I was beyond despair, and so ashamed. After all our success, and after cultivating this so-called perfect 'dream life' I was living, which I knew people envied, I wondered to myself how did I even get to this state of self-loathing, of not wanting any of this? But I knew I would have to get up and keep going, because what else could I do?

All I knew was that I hated myself, I hated Craig, and I hated Triangl. I was, quite clearly, hanging by a thread.

Chapter One

Via the Shop Floor

My dad very proudly likes to tell a story about me, a story which he believes was how he knew I was going to do something special. For me, I reflect on it as being the start of my obsession with business, and the understanding of what it took to make a sale.

I was five years old, and my family was at my sister's primary-school fair. There were bunches of balloons tied up around the school grounds to add a festive atmosphere to the day.

There were lots of little stands selling different things, such as mini soaps, flavoured fudge and cakes. Of course, these items cost money, money my parents weren't willing to hand out to me for no good reason.

In light of this, I had to find a way to get some money and so I walked around, untying all the balloons I could get my hands on and proceeded to walk around the fair, selling individual balloons for 20 cents each. I keenly remember every part of this experience. The surprise and the joy on people's faces when I tried to sell them a balloon. The way I initially felt scared to go up to strangers and talk to them, but that once I did, and smiled, it was the connection that I made with them that convinced them to buy a balloon from me. It was a powerful feeling. Sure, who would say no to a 20-cent balloon being sold to them by a child, but for me it was much more. It made me feel confident, and it filled me with a self-belief that I could get what I wanted in life if I was brave enough to try new things, to seize opportunities where I saw them – to be entrepreneurial.

In Australia, the legal age to be able to work was fourteen years and nine months, and I counted down the days until I was old enough with feverish excitement. I was so excited to grow up, to earn money, to experience new feelings and new challenges.

My first weekend job was at a café, as a waitress. Which I *hated*. The owner, who was the chef, was a highly strung individual which filtered down to the rest of the staff. It was exhausting. I was never properly trained so I was winging it from day one, which isn't so bad when waiting and clearing tables, but they also had me making coffee. I still feel bad for the customers who ever had to drink one of my very burnt coffees.

The café floor was chaotic. This suburban Melbourne café was the only one in that area, so it was slammed from 9am until around 2pm on weekends. I had no idea what I was doing, and used to dread going to work every day but couldn't bear to quit, because on the scale of first-time jobs, being a waitress was a good one, and I didn't want to give up so quickly.

When I look back at this time, my stress was absolutely due to the toxic work environment, and it was my first glimpse at the boss being the one who sets the tone for the rest of the team. Chris was this particular boss's name, and she had a successful catering business on top of the café. She had most likely taken on more work than she could manage. I clearly recall the day she grabbed both handles of a pot that was on the stove, subsequently burning her hands, and wailing at the top of her voice. Of course it would have been painful, no doubt, but her cries were so much more than that. She was exhausted, strung out, over it. The burn was the last straw for her, and for me, and I quit shortly after.

My next part-time job was at a supermarket. I was a checkout chick, and, oh boy, did I love this job. So much about this job was forming who I was turning into as an adult. First and foremost, I had to stand up against questions and comments from everyone in my life as to why I chose to leave a waitressing job, which seemed quite a glamorous job as a teenager, to instead be a supermarket worker, which to my friends didn't hold quite the same cachet. For me, I'd stayed in the café role a few months too long, considering how much I'd hated it. It was only because I knew I'd be judged for leaving that I stayed for longer than I should have.

Facing that criticism, and honouring my own happiness at the tender age of fifteen, was the first time I'd been aware that happiness often meant going against what society tells you will make you happy, and listening to your own inner voice.

As the supermarket was in my suburb, I often saw the parents of my school friends, and was so often asked 'Oh, you work here now?', which I learned quickly was an opportunity to stand by my decision and not shrink away from it.

There was so much I loved about this job. The short hours (three-hour shifts were quite common); the way I was able to revel in my organising skills by packing the bags in categories and ensuring each bag was filled perfectly; and the way I was trained so well and looked after so professionally, which made me feel valued and cared for. But what I loved the absolute most was talking to people and giving them the best service I possibly could. I relished the fact that I could make customers feel good, or at least better than they had before they went through my checkout lane. I felt useful, I felt appreciated, and I was very good at my job, which made me feel special too.

I had people from all walks of life come through my checkout, and I really learned so much about consumer behaviour, seeing what people bought, how they acted, who they were.

It was utterly fascinating. It was also, at times, quite grounding to realise just how tough many people were doing it. It was on Thursdays that the pension payments would be made for the over-sixties and there would be an influx of elderly customers, purchasing their necessities. It was eye-opening to see what people live off, and that so many were totally reliant on government funds. Not that I condone stealing in any way, but I may or may not have forgotten to scan items for these kinds of customers regularly, and I always made sure to have a conversation, give them big smiles and try to show them I cared in my own small way.

I stayed in this job all through high school and for a few months after I graduated Year 12 in 2002. I finished Year 12 with mediocre results. I received a 67.5 as a score, which was out of 100. Not great, but not too bad considering the severe lack of effort and preparation I put into my final exams. In fact, I turned eighteen in the middle of exams, and I was going out to clubs in the middle of the two-week exam period.

I was intelligent enough and considered to be a very 'bright student', but my lack of application to my studies was consistent from the beginning of secondary school at the small independent girls school in Melbourne I attended from Year 7 straight through to Year 12.

During my primary-school years I had attended no less than five primary schools. We moved around Australia because of my dad who was working his way up the management ranks at an insurance company. I had become very used to packing up and moving every few years, and I absolutely loved this part of my life. I was accustomed to being 'the new girl', and absolutely thrived on being one. It gave me a great skill in life: to be able to easily assimilate into different social situations and find connection with strangers. It also gave me a lot of freedom to be whoever I wanted to be and try out different interests and hobbies, based on the friends I was making in different schools.

In primary school, I was always one of the smartest students. I had a natural ability with words and flourished in writing and reading. I also loved and played a lot of sports, which I credit to my father for basically raising me to be a tomboy.

I am the middle child in my family and have an older sister, Bree, and a younger brother, Myles. My parents were supposed to have only two children, and I was supposed to be a boy. My dad was the only male child in his family, and to carry on the Deering name, I needed to be a boy as well. Suffice to say, when I came out a girl, there was a little disappointment, largely from Nanna, my dad's mother, who refused to visit me in hospital or for weeks afterwards, and never really warmed up to me during her time on this earth.

Despite my being very much a girl, I grew up being very much a tomboy, obsessed with cricket, footy, cars and planes – a lot because of my dad's earnest interest in these things. I was such a tomboy that I only received my first doll when I was ten, and from then on embraced the more feminine side of myself.

We grew up as a standard middle-class family, and my childhood was an easy one: I felt safe, looked after and loved all the time. We never went without the things we wanted, within reason, and certainly never without anything we needed. We had a yearly holiday – nothing flashy, usually a trip to another city – and I had a fun and full childhood. In spite of this, I always wanted more. I hated that my friends often had nicer cars, bigger houses, beach houses and seemingly better lives.

My dad, especially, saw this longing in me and always encouraged me to use this desire as fuel to do more with my life.

It was early on in my years at secondary school that it became clear I wasn't going to do very well in this system. I was regularly told 'if only she applied herself, she could do better, she could be better'. I was in a school that favoured maths and science, both areas that I loathed and wasn't naturally good at. The school also acknowledged art, but that wasn't my strength either. I enjoyed drama and English, and so the school very early on categorised me as a student who wasn't likely to get high grades and do the school proud (as so often happens in the education system), and left me to basically fend for myself in regards to getting support or real guidance. I also made no secret of the fact that I had no idea what I wanted to do when I left school.

In Year 10, aged sixteen, much fuss was, and still is, made over meeting the career counsellor to discuss what it was that you wanted to do for the rest of your life. Because, of course, one should know at this age. The age where you are not even an adult, but also not really a child anymore. Possibly one of the most confusing times as a human, but yes, let's choose our career right now!

I made it very clear in these meetings I had absolutely no idea what I wanted to do.

What I liked was words, and I liked people. That was about it. The counsellor came up with a few options: a lawyer, a social worker, a psychologist. All perfectly fine options, but all requiring a high level of academic achievement (social work was the 'in' career of the time so the entry-level marks were in the eighties when it would normally have been in the sixties) – marks I knew I wasn't going to get anywhere near. I hated studying. A true procrastinator, I left everything until the night before, which usually worked okay enough through my years at school, but I knew that when it came to exams cramming wasn't going to cut it.

From Year 10 I resigned myself to knowing I most likely wouldn't get a university degree. This was no doubt frustrating for my parents, who had sacrificed a lot to put me through a private-school education, without any benefit of a university degree to come from it. It was a point of contention for my dad for a while, and he used to often express his frustration over my lack of interest in 'doing well' at school. He saw something in me, as he so often told me, and felt that I was special, that I was 'bright' and that he wanted to see me use my brains as I was destined to.

While this sometimes showed up in him as frustration towards me, it was my dad who gave me my unwavering self-belief. He made me believe I was able to be whoever I wanted to be, and do whatever I wanted to do, if I worked hard enough at it. By stamping a work ethic in me, at every chance he got, my dad saved me from pursuing a pointless uni degree and led to me deciding to work full time as soon as I left school instead.

Dad had a particular interest in a man called Charlie Bell and he would tell me his story often. Charlie was the first ever non-American and also the youngest person to be the global CEO of McDonald's. Charlie started at McDonald's when he was just fifteen, and worked his way up to be the big boss through the stores' ranks.

This story, and Dad's belief in me, made me feel anything was possible, and once I finished school, I decided to jump into the industry I was into most at the time, and work my way up, Charlie Bell-style.

That industry was fashion, and the way into it was via the shop floor.

I had been interested in a career in fashion buying – just like any young woman obssessed with fashion – but as my Year 12 results weren't high enough to get me into a marketing or business degree at a reputable university, I was going to have to find another way in.

It was hard to get on to the shop floor in retail. Every place I looked required experience, which I of course didn't have. After a month of looking anywhere and everywhere, I found a temporary casual role for a costume-jewellery brand, who were setting up a Christmas pop-up store at a shopping centre. They didn't require experience, and I jumped at the opportunity, knowing this would give me the experience I needed for the real 'fashion' stores.

The store I was in was not a whole store, more a slice of a store in a corner of the shopping centre. But I was happy. My résumé was expanding!

I had to wear a uniform every day, a white t-shirt emblazoned with '3 for $10' on both front and back. I was quite literally signage for the store, but I didn't mind as it allowed me to befriend some guys from the surfwear store next door, who wanted to buy the t-shirts to wear out at night to the clubs, and so we struck up a friendship, which then extended to my getting to know the girls in the store next to them – a women's clothing store.

It didn't take long for a role to come up with them – staff turnover is always high in retail. The role was for an assistant store manager, and as I was technically store manager of the '3 for $10' store (it actually didn't have a name), I was able to bluff my way into the role.

From there, I jumped from retail store to retail store. It took me a while to get to store manager, but, once there, it then became a matter of finding the right fit. I learned fast that the toxicity of the retail fashion space made my first café role seem absolutely mild in comparison. Retail was dominated by young women, and it felt often like a high-school playground in terms of the gossip and the bitchiness.

I had to learn very quickly to stay as removed from it all as possible, and focus solely on the work at hand, namely the customers, to ensure I didn't end up becoming embroiled in the latest drama.

I moved around in the next few years to a few different companies, all in fashion retail. I was trying to find the perfect fit, the perfect culture, the perfect place. I tried smaller, more 'fashion' brands, like Bettina Liano, Roy and Bardot, and I tried the big national companies, namely Sportsgirl, Witchery and even Supré.

While at the time it was a bit disheartening, as none of the places seemed the right fit for me, I was benefiting from the experience of all these varied workplaces, with all their different practices, cultures, customers. This was going to serve me well in future years, when it came to starting my own business, although that wasn't even factoring into my wildest of dreams back in those retail days.

I'd decided after perhaps my third or fourth role on the floor that I wanted to get into head office of one of those companies. I wanted to go behind the scenes. The ceiling wasn't very high in the retail roles. I had no interest in becoming an area, state or national manager, as I felt it only would mean more politics, more toxicity. I'd had many area managers in my time as a store manager, and they were usually girls or women on a total power trip, coming in weekly and causing absolute chaos in the stores, and creating a very negative workplace. I wanted to be far away from that, and felt it was much safer in the head offices. I didn't really care how I got in or what role I would take, I just wanted in.

It was not long after this realisation that I had an opportunity to travel overseas for the first time. Well, not true; I'd been to Bali. But this was different – I had friends moving to London, a bit of a rite of passage for many a young Australian. I got it into my head one night that I needed to go on this trip. A mere eight weeks later I was on a plane, indeed moving to London. I had always been an act-now-think-later kind of person, and once my mind was made up, it was well and truly made up. I saved as much money as I could in those eight weeks, and with the plan to work as soon as I got to London, I left Melbourne.

I only stayed for six months, from March through September 2007, and I worked temp office roles to get me by just enough to be able to visit Paris, Amsterdam, Croatia and Greece. A very typical expat experience, with several phone calls back home to Mum and Dad in those months, pleading to borrow yet another small amount of money to get me through.

I returned home to Australia with a renewed drive to get my career going. I'd had enough of a taste of the world, I'd seen the lives some people lived, and I just wanted to grow up and get going with being a real adult, with a real job.

I was twenty-three when I got back to Melbourne, and, with a ton of retail experience and absolutely zero office experience, I sought a role in a head office. I didn't care where the role was based within Melbourne, or what the title was, as long as it was within a company that sold consumer products and I was directly involved with those products.

Still, almost all of those roles required direct experience or a university degree, neither of which I had. After weeks of job-searching, I found a marketing assistant role, and while it did ask for marketing experience or a uni degree, it said 'preferred' over 'must have'. I wrote the most convincing cover letter I possibly could and, after interviewing with a few people within the company, I was hired.

The business was a costume-jewellery wholesale brand. They made all the costume jewellery for the biggest retailers in Australia, and it was only a 25-minute drive from my home. I was still living with my parents, with no plans yet to move, as was becoming quite normal with my generation.

While my title was 'marketing assistant', I was directly reporting to one of the senior buyers, Philip, and was essentially his assistant. He was older, in his late forties, and had been working at the company for years.

Philip was quite direct and snappy to other colleagues in the office at times, but he loved me and took me under his wing, teaching me all I could ever want to know in terms of development and design. Being a buyer was the dream for most young girls working in fashion. Quarterly trips to Europe and the US were what we all dreamed about, and it seemed so glamorous and elevated. My three years working with Philip undid all the glamour of this industry, as we both spent 80 per cent of our time on Microsoft Excel.

I learned quickly that, largely, Australian fashion design meant reinventing what was bought overseas on buying trips. This was the Aussie way, as we were always behind the European season by six months, which meant whatever they were releasing was what we could release shortly after.

Samples bought overseas were rife in the office, and making our own version of them was the way it was. It was to never look exactly the same, but similar. Philip handled this carefully and with integrity, and sought my advice as time went on. Before long, I was developing ranges and collections with him.

I learned, for the first time, all about the critical path, which was the timeline of a design being drawn up, then samples initiated with our manufacturers, straight through to the arrival into store. This process was my first experience of seeing what it was like to deal with Chinese manufacturers, and how samples were so often incorrect the first and second time, and how you had to very carefully monitor the whole process to ensure quality matched the cost price we were given by the manufacturers. Philip had been in the industry for decades and knew intimately how it worked. He knew when a design didn't match the price given or something was off, and he taught me how and why he picked up on certain things. He was tough but fair – he'd have heated arguments with Adrian, the chain-smoking head of supply chain, over shoddy samples and production delays, but then continue on kindly with him later. He never held a grudge or made things personal – something I'd never seen in my years working in retail – and this cemented in me how to act in the workplace, and how to not avoid conflict as it often meant getting the best result, if handled professionally.

I stayed with Phillip for three years, but started getting itchy feet. I wanted more, again. I wanted to take my knowledge, and my now fairly strong level of experience, at least for a 25-year- old, and try working for a national company. This was where I thought I'd climb the ranks, and be able to at least become a buyer within a year or two.

I took a role as a production-development assistant at Myer, Australia's largest retailer, in the underwear department, right next to fashion. I was getting closer to where I wanted to be.

The office was brand-new and in the city, and it felt exciting, like I was a real adult.

While my role with the jewellery wholesaler was extremely hands-on, my role at Myer was not. Being a large company meant roles were very defined and there wasn't much movement outside of them. I spent my days inputting orders into the computer system, and occasionally assisting the senior buyer on range-showing days. It was hideously boring. I tried to tell myself this was all for a bigger cause, and that I would be able to be promoted far easier in a company this size. But, at the end of the day, it was a corporate company, and it was absolutely not suited to me. This was quite a big realisation, but one I was grateful to have experienced early on in my career. By the time I quit, only five months into the job, my desire to be a buyer had completely evaporated, and instead I turned my focus to the new world growing rapidly online.

It was around 2010 that Australian consumer-led businesses were starting to look to the internet as a real commodity for their brands and beginning to open 'online stores'.

This was extremely exciting for me, as I'd realised a few things during my short tenure at Myer. Firstly, I missed customer interaction. I missed actually being able to get their feedback, understand who they were, what they were buying and why. Secondly, I preferred small business. Ones where I was able to understand the operations easier and be a part of them too.

With these new-found realisations at the forefront of my mind, I put my feelers out to discover which businesses were looking at opening an online store.

An ex-colleague of mine at one of the smaller retailers I had worked for, Teale, had gone out on her own and started a clothing brand called Friends of Mine. It was Melbourne based, cute party and daywear, and doing fairly well. (NB: Teale is now behind the cool girl label Réalisation Par.) They were slowly opening an online store, but needed to give autonomy to someone to run it so she and her co-founder could focus on the growth of the brand. I'd never wanted a job more in my life, and I could not believe it when I was offered the role.

It was essentially managing a store, but from the office. Without any bitchy girls or toxic environment. It was just myself and my customer. It truly felt like the dream job.

I was so in love with the premise behind online stores – the idea that you could shop privately, whenever you wanted. That you could lie on your bed after work and pick an outfit for the weekend, or choose presents for friends in the comfort and privacy of your own space – it was the greatest evolving landscape I'd ever witnessed, let alone been a part of.

I loved being in charge of my space. Of being able to nurture these girls buying the pieces. Picking and packing their orders, following up with them when I felt it was right to. Going above and beyond to build a community. I believed so much in the way this was going to make so many people feel good, to get a package from me, with an item I'd often helped them choose via email chats, and a handwritten note. It came so naturally to me because it felt like such a relief to be able to do this every day with no other distractions.

As the business was small, I was also able to advise the co-founders on customer behaviour as it unfolded in front of me. I'd be able to mention that a particular style was perhaps fitting wrong as it had been returned more times than other styles or advise on making more of a style as it was selling out super-fast and being requested over and over again. The brand was able to have such control over what they were doing because of this rapid feedback process and total visibility over what was going on.

It really did seem like online stores and consumer products were a match made in heaven, in terms of being able to be super-reactive to consumer behaviour in relation to their specific offerings.

An unfortunate experience at this company – in which one of the co-founders read my personal emails on my company-owned laptop, in which my current boyfriend and I were ironically bitching over the co-founder in question's tendency to act in an unprofessional manner, and fired me on the spot one afternoon (she did try to re-hire me days later but it was enough unprofessionalism to call it a day from my side) – was unable to deter me from the love I had for the space, and, shortly after, I found a similar role with another company.

In every interaction I had with a customer, I treated them as if they were Customer Number One. The boss. In my eyes, this customer was our best chance for growing a brand. I knew the power in customer service, in great customer service. I'd lived and breathed it for ten years by this point. I'd gotten to know the nuances of what made a customer want to buy something. Even over email, I sought it out as my primary task, to work out what they really wanted and give it to them. And, of course, it was more than the actual item they'd ordered. How many people just buy for no reason? There was *always* a reason. And I took great joy in connecting with my customers over their *why*. And working out how to support them in feeling good. It was as simple and as complex as that and I obsessed over it, day and night.

I used to imagine their faces, opening their package and finding their purchase, and smiling because the whole process was flawless. I was so fuelled when I'd often receive an email from a customer to just say thank you. The times I was told they'd never experienced service like that before were what drove me to keep caring the way I was.

I was equally as driven by the negative emails. The ones in which their shipment didn't arrive in time or at all, a bikini was faulty, the sizing was wrong – standard issues an online business faces. Initially these hurt to read, and I'd often cry with frustration over the fact I'd not delivered a 10/10 experience. But as was the case in my retail days, the opportunity to win over a customer who'd had a negative experience was one not to be missed. I went above and beyond with these customers, first by validating their frustrations, which disarmed the majority, and then solving their problem in any way I could.

My love for my customers was simply based on how I wanted to feel and be treated.

I remember those days as a teenager, walking into fashion stores and feeling like eyes were on you, and you were being judged for simply being there. It was an early promise to myself that I would never be like that when I worked in fashion. I would never use it as an excuse to be mean or rude or exclusionary.

The simple promise I made to myself was to always think of the customer as if it was me in their shoes, with everything I did and every decision I made. The customer always comes first.

Chapter Two

A Gap in the Market

Craig and I met in 2011, a day after my twenty-seventh birthday. He was ten years older than me, so I was immediately intimidated and equally flattered when he showed interest in me. I knew of him; of course I did – an ex-AFL footballer, who'd founded a very cool t-shirt label after his footy days. He was quite the Melbourne socialite, and I instantly recognised him the night I met him, at a girlfriend's birthday party in Prahran, the night after my own twenty-seventh birthday. In fact, I'd openly voiced many years prior, many times over, that I'd end up with a very tall, dark, handsome man one day – a man who had played professional football but worked in fashion. An odd combination for back in the early 2000s, and one I felt seemed like a dream come true if it manifested! In years to come, I wondered if I'd indeed dreamed up this man to come into my life. On reflection, I wish I'd manifested less material attributes, not striving for someone as professionally and personally accomplished, as a lot about this dream man wasn't quite what my young self was ready for.

Craig pursued me strongly after that night, in a way I'd never been pursued before, calling me the day after we met, with a cute recollection of the pony hair mini skirt I was wearing that first night, and arranging our first date for that coming Tuesday. I was absolutely under his spell. Our first date was a few days after our initial meeting. I caught the train into the city, as living pay cheque to pay cheque didn't lend itself kindly to a taxi ride. It was this first date that set the tone for all to come, and it is a date I can recall with every fibre of my being.

I fell instantly for Craig, his 193-centimetre height and extremely impressive body being obvious characteristics, but which in combination with his delicate, softly spoken nature made him irresistible to me. I was so inspired by everything he'd done, having played AFL for over a decade, founded a successful t-shirt brand and trained to be a commercial pilot, to name the highlights, and everything he stood for, in terms of his honesty and accountability over his failings so far in his thirty-eight years. He seemed so spiritual, so calm, so interesting, and he was interested in me – a regular 27-year-old born-and-bred Melbourne girl, with no formal qualifications, no self-confidence and no bloody idea what the hell she was doing. I was ambitious as hell, but had nowhere to place my ambition. And Craig, having lived a decade more than me, a hugely informative decade – one I was about to learn much about! – felt like a safe place to invest myself in. And so I did. That first night, at a Thai restaurant in Melbourne's CBD, we spent hours talking about our lives thus far, who we wanted to be and why we wanted to be more than we were. It wasn't a normal first date for me. I felt like I belonged to him, and that whatever he wanted to do was what we would do together.

I can't write a book on my Triangl story without including the second date – the story I have told over and over and with such insistence that this was the moment Triangl was born. The real truth of it is that by the second date, I was already so invested in the new identity I was forming with Craig that it didn't matter what was coming – I was going to agree to anything he wanted us to do.

When you're a young woman dating a man who is a whole ten years older than you and who you're really into, you are often fairly vulnerable. When you're a young woman dating an older man who suggests the beach as a location for your second date, you're terrified at the prospect of feeling as physically exposed as you already are emotionally!

If you know me, you know this story. If you're new here, the story goes like this: Craig suggested the beach, Half Moon Bay in Brighton, Melbourne, as the spot to spend the afternoon. I'm not a bikini girl – shock horror, the co-founder of Triangl didn't even really like swimwear! – but I'm a fashion girl. So I wanted to look good. And my Cotton On black bikini wasn't going to cut it. So, I spent a few panicked hours on a Saturday morning rushing around Chadstone Shopping Centre to find a bikini. And I couldn't find a bloody thing. It was either surf brands like Roxy, Billabong or Quiksilver, which didn't cut it in terms of prints and shapes. Or it was Zimmermann, whose bikinis were sitting at a pretty $155 a set, which was basically my entire fortnight's disposable income.

I became acutely aware of a complete lack of any cool, fashionable-looking bikinis under $100. I was an old retail girl by trade, and had a fair understanding of customer psychology and interest by this stage, combined with a total love for all things fashion and clothing, so I knew a big gap in the market when I could see it – and this was it!

I took this information, along with my $155 Zimmermann bikini – hey, a girl has to dress to impress – and proceeded to tell Craig all about my morning adventure.

I expected him to be impressed by my market awareness, but wasn't quite expecting his fervour at the idea of making bikinis ourselves. I'd never entertained starting a business before. I was a very career-driven girl with a ton of ambition but no real desire to start my own brand. I was still working my life out. I was playing it safe, working for a small business to understand it all before I ever dipped my toe into my own thing. I can't even honestly say I ever would have started my own business. I was very interested in the so-called freedom of working for myself. Not being a slave to the nine to five, or having a boss – all the usual things. But I felt like I was too young to know what I even wanted to do yet. I felt I had a lot more growing up to do before I did something as adult as starting a business.

However, this was not Craig's way of being. He'd had a business. He was bankrupt when we met, which I remember him telling me early on, although I can't quite recall when as it felt like such an insignificant part of who he was. It was simply something that had happened to him, and he explained the bankruptcy so openly that it didn't faze me at all. He was the first person I'd ever even met who was bankrupt, and because of his apparent integrity and worldliness, it really shaped my opinion of bankruptcy in business. It felt like he'd just been through a lot, it felt like he'd made mistakes that we all have made or will make in life, but he had just been caught out by some significant ones, in terms of timing mainly. What I didn't really realise at the time was that Craig was focused on launching a new business, and applying the lessons from the mistakes he had made, to ensure its success, or at least ensuring it wasn't impacted by the same mistakes as last time.

To this day, I see bankruptcy as a blessing to those in business who have been through it. To those who overcame fear and had a real go at making something work. The lessons I saw Craig apply to Triangl as a result of his bankruptcy were hugely formative in the setup of our business, and I am inspired by anyone who has been through a failure and uses it to push forward once again.

After our second date, this defining day for the genesis of Triangl, our romantic relationship continued to grow, alongside our business relationship. I am a hopeless romantic – I love love, and being in love – so my focus was on nurturing this side of us, while Craig was far more focused on the Triangl version of us and continued to move forward with the setup of a brand. These experiences initially set the tone for Craig and me. He was always the most loving and most happy when creating, and discussing design with me. He didn't want to differentiate our personal relationship from our work relationship, which I resented almost immediately. I always wanted to split the two. To have a work–life balance, to have a date night where we kept work at work and talked about everything or anything else. But this wasn't of much interest to him, and I could tell I got so much more from him when we spoke about Triangl, so I obliged and adapted to his way of being – and, in turn, began to abandon my own.

With both of us working full-time jobs, Craig as a denim designer for a manufacturing company, and me in ecommerce customer care, it was usually at night where we would sit and map out the infancy of the brand, him at his desk and me on the bed. (I'd moved in to his house in Brighton over the summer.) The logo, the name, the initial designs. The name was a simple enough process. We wanted a niche, so our original plan was to do a 70s-style triangle bikini. A string bikini top and a little hipster bottom. It was all I wore at the time, and it was the style Craig liked the most too, so it was a no-brainer to focus on that shape at the start. I'd worked enough in the industry to assert that a niche product was easier to market for a totally new and unknown brand. Keeping it simple would appeal to an impulse-buying mentality. It would create a talking point among friends: 'Have you seen the brand that makes the triangle bikinis? It's called Triangl.'

We dropped the 'e' at the end of the word – reason being it was going to be impossible to register the name 'Triangle' anywhere globally, as the name was already ubiquitous, but also it would have been hard to search us on the internet as 'Triangle' and actually find our brand, again because it is such a common word. Triangl would be an easy one to find, while sounding exactly the same as the original word.

Funnily enough, I despised the word! For so long I felt such embarrassment saying it. It was quite masculine and direct and made me feel uncomfortable. I've said 'triangle without the e' more times than I can even fathom. But, like all things in life that hang around for a while, I grew to love it, eventually.

We had the name, we had the style, we also had a logo. Another conscious decision we made was to keep our logo black and white. The less aligned to a colour we were, the more wide-ranging appeal we had. I'm all for colour, personally. And our intention was to definitely make bikinis in colours but to appeal to as many people as possible, and while we were working out who we were as a brand, black and white was the choice.

All this part of building a brand identity felt fun. I remember it felt like a big game of 'pretend'. Let's pick a logo! A name! A style! It was all creative, with no real skin in the game of putting a product out to market. At this point, everything works – you're making decisions on your foundational business markers in bed at 10pm, where it all seems fanciful, hopeful and even a little bit silly. I definitely didn't see Triangl going anywhere at this point. It felt like a fun side project of flippant creation. I was trying hard to accelerate my career, working in ecommerce as a customer care and development manager at a Melbourne based company called Green with Envy. Initially the place to go for a formal dress, GWE had since become a multi-brand retail store, stocking the likes of Alexander Wang, Zimmermann, Nicholas, and Camilla and Marc, and were moving into taking it all online. These were days where online was a luxury, just a new option to sell fashion from. Not a necessity, just something different, where sales could be occasionally procured by a girl sitting on her bed at night on her work laptop.

My years in retail sales and interest in customer behaviour naturally led to the ecomm space. I loved being able to find ways to draw a customer to buy a dress from her favourite shop while she was at home. It felt so smart, because it's how I wanted to shop. I was working all week long, and having only two nights a week to go to the stores felt too restrictive.

At the time Craig and I were working on Triangl's initial launch, Green with Envy were setting up an online store (eboutique as it was known then) and had brought me in to set up the customer-facing side of the store. It was this experience that drove Craig and me to move to an online-only model fairly quickly (although we did briefly dabble in the wholesale space after launch, as a means to market the brand and use physical retail spaces as a tool for people to see us and then come and find us online).

As focused as I was on my full-time job, I knew there was a ceiling that I was fast approaching. In the short months since Craig and I had met, my eyes had been opened to the world of the entrepreneur. The allure of having no boss, no set hours, and no expectations from management started to seem like the goal, and Craig and I started planning how to make Triangl really happen.

To launch a product, you first need one. We'd worked on a handful of initial designs, all in one shape, the standard-issue triangle bikini, which was all I ever wore at the time, and all that Craig liked me to wear as well. It was really the main reason behind our brand name. Our first style was not made of the neoprene for which we became famous, but a standard bikini fabric that was an 80/20 blend of nylon and spandex.

Craig had already been involved with manufacturing in China and had built good relationships with agents and manufacturers – enough to draw up a tech pack and have a sample made. This was a lengthy process in early 2012, and often took up weeks of our time. We'd email off a tech pack, receive a physical sample to fit perhaps two weeks later, make fit changes, email them back and repeat. With all our commitments, there was limited time we could spend on the business, and it seemed like we'd be years off launching a brand we were proud of.

With this in mind, after visiting Hong Kong in April 2012 as part of his role at the time as a designer for a denim brand, Craig returned home to announce his plans for us both to make the move to Hong Kong, not only because it was closer to Chinese manufacturers, but it was also taking us away from any of the potential distractions of our reasonably comfortable life in Melbourne.

I'd never even visited Hong Kong before, and it wasn't a city on my radar in any way, shape or form. However, it was not really up to me (in my mind, anyway). By this stage, I'd already begun to isolate myself from my friends, something I was prone to doing in romantic relationships, and this helped me process the move overseas as I was already fully invested in our life together, as just the two of us. The thought of quitting our jobs and moving to another country felt terrifyingly exciting. At the time, I didn't think too much into the future, other than the feeling of complete trust and blind faith in the decision Craig was making for us – and for Triangl.

At the time, I had been suffering from an eating disorder for a number of years, which had started after a break-up when I was twenty-four. I had told Craig of my bulimia fairly early on in our relationship. The intimacy of sharing my hopes and dreams, as well as my problems, with Craig meant I felt extremely tied to him because of all he knew and accepted about me. I also had an idealistic view of leaving behind the 'old me' in Melbourne and starting afresh in Hong Kong. I felt perhaps I could be happy and healthy over there, and that leaving Melbourne would mean leaving my mental and physical issues there too.

It was an easy decision to say yes to the move, and get over there as quickly as possible.

I resigned from my job the very next day. The easiest resignation of my life, with the excuse 'I'm moving overseas'. I remember feeling so excited, yet frustrated by the lack of excitement of those around me. My boss at the time told me I was just about to receive a large promotion within the business and asked if I really wanted to go overseas for no reason. My close friends were the same, and my family too, although, knowing me the best, they weren't going to get in my way when I'd made up my mind.

It felt like no one believed in me, and while perhaps that was helpful because it gave me the drive to get over there and succeed, at the time it felt awful to feel these snippets of doubt from those around me.

Craig and I sold all we had in those five short weeks before we left. Listing items on eBay during the week and having them collected all weekend long was how we spent our last weeks in Australia. At the end, we had about $10,000. Enough for the flights over there, to pay for the rent of a small studio apartment for a few months, and other necessary living costs.

Those last few weeks in Melbourne felt largely hopeful. I was doing something no one else I'd known had done. I was moving to another country, to turn a dream into a reality. It sounded so romantic! Deep down, though, I was desperately battling with my mental health. The natural fears I had about this monumental move were being pushed into the back of my mind. I remember bringing up my fears once with Craig, a mere week out from our planned departure, and his reaction being so inflamed at my even mentioning any doubts over the move, that I immediately retracted what I had said, and didn't bring it up again, with him or anyone else.

My inability – or lack of freedom – to verbalise what was a completely normal thought process was extremely detrimental. It set the tone for how I communicated with Craig from here on out. I kept my fears buried deep down, not only as we proceeded with the launch of Triangl, but for years to come. This lack of communication and expression perpetuated my eating disorder, so that it became even more of a crutch I used to feel some sort of control when I wanted to express myself and felt I couldn't, or shouldn't, for fear of conflict.

All of this came down to my complete lack of sense of self, and not having done any self-development work. I was a 27-year-old, in an intimate and working relationship with a man ten years my senior, moving countries with him to start a business, without any clarity about how that would look and feel because I hadn't developed a mental-health toolkit for myself yet. That girl I was needed some guidance and support, and was going it totally alone.

I remember I had arranged a dinner with my best school friends, the night before we flew out. Craig and I were ready to get on that plane, packed and all, and our imminent departure was feeling all too real in those last moments at our home, so I was flustered on my way to dinner. I arrived late, and so was seated at the end of the table. It made me feel like a bit of an afterthought rather than the guest of honour, so I was perhaps not as engaging as I usually was at social events. Midway through the dinner, which was reasonably enjoyable by then, we got to talking about my adventure ahead, and I played into the idealistic dream awaiting me. My new life, with my inspirational boyfriend, where the sky was the limit and success was inevitable. All was going well until my girlfriend Carli chimed in with a cutting statement. 'I don't know, babe, but this feels wrong – this doesn't feel good. Are you sure you want to go away with him? We don't even know this guy!'

I'll never ever forget this moment because it felt like she'd seen my soul, and she *knew*. I wasn't ready to go away like this. I was scared. What if we failed? What if I let him down? What if he knew I wasn't any good at anything at all?

I bit back, in classic Erin form (I'm a Scorpio rising after all!), and assured her I was in love and we were going to do something great, something special, together. And at the end I added in to appease her – and to calm myself down – that I could always just come home if I wanted to. I was a mere plane ride away.

I knew I had to go; I knew I needed to do it. My resolve was strong, and I still had enough self-belief at this point to know I wanted something special for my life and that I had to go and make it happen, even if it might break me in the process.

Craig picked me up after this dinner and I didn't mention what had transpired. Instead, I made a mental note to not talk to those friends again for a while. Keep them at arm's length. I couldn't handle being questioned, so avoidance was key.

The next day, 3 June 2012, we left wintry Melbourne for hot, sticky, sweaty Hong Kong to start our new lives – to start Triangl.

Chapter Three

A Brand-new Life and a New Brand

We arrived in Hong Kong in peak typhoon season, which meant cloudy days, regular downpours and the stickiest heat you could imagine. It could have felt suffocating but it felt exciting to me. It was just so different to what we'd left in Melbourne, and it was so refreshing to be somewhere else, doing something so different with my life .

The first weeks were more akin to a holiday. I was settling in, discovering the city, trying to assimilate as quickly as possible. To me, Hong Kong was a fascinating city, like nowhere else in the world. A mix of local Hong Kong residents, expats from all over the globe, usually in finance, mixed in with Chinese mainlanders and everyone else. A global 'anonymous' city, as I liked to call it, where you could be whoever you truly wanted to be, and not feel judged or exposed. I fell in love with the city immediately.

In these initial weeks of romanticising Hong Kong, Craig moved quickly on proposing, swiftly finding a rather large fake diamond from a jeweller on Kowloon Island and taking me to a very fancy sky-high bar called Ozone, 118 floors up, to get on one knee for half a second and ask me if I'd marry him. It was a mildly romantic moment, if not one

I completely expected after our move together to another country. My strongest memory from that day, however, is how we were greeted with grey clouds, and I even wondered back then if it would be an ominous sign for our future.

Our little apartment was in Central, Hong Kong. It was right below Hollywood Road, which I'd been briefed was *the* street in Hong Kong. It didn't really feel too vibey at all, to be honest, but I soon learned and understood the definition of the cool places in Hong Kong. It was more that these areas were the ones frequented by the Aussies, Americans, Brits, French and Spaniards. They were the bulk of the expats around Central at the time. We lived right below Soho, a little section next to the famous escalator, where everyone hung out, all night, every night. The culture of the city was absolutely work hard, play hard – and everyone seemed to be there to have a good time.

We spent our first week in a little hotel, waiting for the bed we had ordered to arrive at our apartment. The room was so unbelievably small and uncomfortable that I was incredibly impressed, in contrast, by the time I first set eyes on our apartment. We had gotten lucky. Most expats lived in those multi-storey apartment buildings that housed hundreds, if not thousands, of people. They were nice enough, but very soulless and carbon copies of one another. Our apartment was in an amazing spot, right in the heart of Central. Setting us back around US$1000 per month, it was a small building with four levels. No elevator, just a staircase at the back. Climbing four levels numerous times a day in the Hong Kong humidity was a workout in itself. The sweat that poured out when doing those steps was outrageous and something I'll never forget. And when we started to travel, we had to do it with suitcases! A real punish, but it was worth it for the spaciousness of our apartment. There were only eight apartments in the building, and we had one other family on our level. Our apartment itself had been painted white, and was a bare-bones shell of a place, which suited our aesthetic perfectly. We were able to fit in our bed, a TV cabinet, a desk, a few racks of clothing and some shelving. There were big windows on every wall that looked down to the little street below and gave us beautiful, natural light. We had trees to look out at, and we had a few little restaurants on our street too (one which was a renowned Michelin-recommended Hong Kong restaurant, specialising in tomato noodle soup). We also had no less than three air conditioners for a space no bigger than 15 square metres. Sure, our kitchen was so small we needed to walk sideways to get into it, our toilet quite literally sat below our showerhead (handy for cleaning the toilet daily!), and we had no hot water – only a water heater that needed fifteen minutes to heat up, and only lasted for between five and ten minutes. But I knew the universe had our back in this space. It felt almost too good to be true to be in such a lovely, open space. And it was why we stayed in that apartment for almost two years, even after we could have afforded to move somewhere a lot nicer. We really did love it there. It was our way to feel so part of the city while staying indoors almost 24/7 to get Triangl off the ground.

It took six months in Hong Kong before we had a product to sell. After our initial weeks of assimilation into the city, which involved a lot of eating and a lot of drinking, we got to work. Well, Craig did anyway. My level of experience in retail and ecommerce wasn't serving us at all at this point, and my days were rather empty.

I'd walk every morning, up to the Peak (the most punishing set of hills I've ever seen!), and then return to find Craig designing or creating samples. He wasn't just working on Triangl at this point but also on one of his friend's new brands – silk activewear. Our savings were depleting rapidly, and to even contemplate placing an order for Triangl with a manufacturer meant we needed more money.

Craig's involvement with this silk brand was because of our need to do something else as a way of earning an income, but as we both were unable to work legally, this job was the only thing he could sneakily do. He was being paid very little, not even enough to live off (as we were soon to find out), but it was our only choice. We were almost finished with samples for Triangl, and were in a holding pattern of waiting while we found the funds to initiate the business. We essentially parked Triangl for a few months while trying to get the money to move it forward.

I had nothing to do in these months, essentially. I was missing home terribly and feeling absolutely useless. I wasn't able to work in Hong Kong as I had no visa to allow for it, and I felt incredibly stuck and, in my fragile state, very resentful towards Craig in this process. Feeling like I had no control over my scenario led to me developing an extremely anorexic way of being. It was easy to do so; I was alone for most of the day so could be totally consumed with avoiding my hunger. We didn't have much money, so I wasn't even able to afford to eat heaps, and I played into this as much as possible. I would have walked 15 to 20 kilometres a day, which was always a punishing act as well. The time spent obsessing over my weight and avoiding food consumed those first months in Hong Kong. Of course, it showed up in many other toxic ways, which, back then, I never linked to the complete starvation my body and mind were suffering from. When Craig and I ventured out for a drink or dinner, it always ended in vitriol from me aimed at him. Whether it was fuelled by quickly downed cocktails on an empty stomach or by the guilt for having eaten an actual meal at dinner, it was consistent on a 'date night', which we used to have every Friday, and which became such an issue between us due to my rage that it resulted in those evenings becoming few and far between, and then completely non-existent in subsequent years.

Those nights were a release for me, the only release I had. I was homesick, starving myself and without any kind of purpose during the day. It made for a chaotic mind, and one that unravelled easily after any alcohol consumption. These issues I was facing weren't monumental really, on paper. They read like quite common problems for twenty-somethings. But without anyone to talk to, without any connection – they felt huge. They were huge, to me. They sent me spiralling into shame, day after day after day. I felt nothing but discomfort in my own body, and felt so stuck. Both logistically, by being in Hong Kong, and in my own mind. It was the most hopeless I'd ever felt.

After a few months of Craig trying to make this other business opportunity something worthwhile, he made the decision to leave. It had become a full-time role for him, and was not making enough to even cover rent and food let alone a production run for our bikinis. We both still believed Triangl was our best bet and why we had moved over to Hong Kong anyway.

Back in Melbourne, several months prior to us meeting, Craig had collaborated with a small blogger on a collection of coloured denim jeans. The partnership fell through and Craig had been left with the entire order of these jeans, hundreds of pairs. We were almost out of money and with rent and bills constantly looming, we decided we had to try to sell as many as we could. We found a model one afternoon on the street. This wasn't hard as Hong Kong was crawling with models, being a hub for models all over the world who came in hopes of scoring very well-paid jobs for the scores of Hong Kong and Chinese companies seeking Western women. We offered her the collection of jeans, which was six or seven pairs, alongside some images for her portfolio, and she agreed. Craig had dabbled in photography years prior, and was very skilled at it, and in fact, he was the one who shot almost every single Triangl shoot for the first two years. He still had a great camera, and we shot the 'campaign' one night at the bar we regularly frequented, in their upstairs area. With these images, we then hustled to sell as many pairs as we could. I messaged everyone I knew on Facebook, offering the jeans at $40 a pair. We weren't getting much of a reply rate, and without chasing anyone and looking more desperate than we clearly already were, we had come to a roadblock.

Hong Kong is littered with small shopfronts offering printing services, and at a very cheap cost. Craig came up with the idea to print cards to sell the denim, and hand them out on the streets of Hong Kong. The fear this sent through my body is something I can still feel to this day. Not only were we completely broke, and completely devoid of any success whatsoever, we had to stand in public, handing out cards to try and make a dollar.

It was the most humiliating prospect of my life, and one I just couldn't be a part of. I already felt like such a failure; it seemed like I may as well be handing out cards saying, 'I am a joke of a human.' Craig, on the other hand, already had such an entrepreneurial mindset that he didn't care what anyone thought – he just wanted to succeed. I learned so much that day about what it actually takes to run a business, to be an entrepreneur. How you have to park all your ego, and practise total humility in order to prove yourself, and ultimately have the best chance at success. I used this moment of letting my fear beat me to drive me to overcome fear in all other business interactions from then on.

Mind you, Craig didn't sell a single pair of jeans from his hustle on the streets. But that was neither here nor there in my mind, as it was such a pivotal moment in terms of showing me what it took to get anywhere in life. And naturally it caused yet another moment of self-loathing for me, which buried itself into my mind.

With denim sales virtually non-existent, our intention to use that money to launch Triangl was over. It was September 2012. I don't recall the exact date, but I remember it was around AFL finals time, as the footy was on in every pub in Hong Kong. We sat on the steps outside Coast, a popular pub in Central, adjacent to the escalator, as all the best pubs were. To passers-by we would have looked like just another couple sitting having a chat, not a couple deciding on their entire future.

We were out of money. We had no money coming in. We were stuck, or screwed I would say, at this point. Often these types of discussions between Craig and me were heated and, at times, nasty. But not this one. We both were at the mercy of everything that had happened to this point, and here we were. We either flew home to Melbourne and took full-time jobs, or we stayed. Both required money though; we didn't even have enough to fly home with. With this in mind, and knowing we needed to ask for money whichever way we looked at it, we decided we had no choice but to reach out to our nearest and dearest and ask for some actual cash to get Triangl started and continue with our dream.

We needed to be realistic about the money we asked for. Our initial $10,000 on arrival in Hong Kong got us nowhere. So we needed more. Not a wild amount, but enough to put Triangl into the market, and for us to live off for six months without relying too heavily on making immediate sales.

Our rough calculations led us to realising we needed an amount somewhere in between AU$20,000 to 30,000. Asking for money was an easy process by this point, because we had absolutely no other option. We couldn't borrow from a bank as we had no credit, and we couldn't get jobs as we had no working visa.

We asked family first, mine and Craig's. Everyone said no, which was what we expected. I understood why – it all felt too far-fetched and frivolous. None of my friends were financially in a position to lend us any money; there was no one I could have reasonably even asked. 'Come home and start again from Melbourne, with a job behind you' was the sentiment, and this made perfect and logical sense, but we'd come too far to go back at this point.

However, Craig had a few best friends from his footy days who were doing very well financially and were our last and best shot at a loan. Craig asked three of his best friends, and two of them said yes, they could give us some money. On the spot. With no questions asked. Of course, it was a loan, so we promised to pay them back as soon as we were able. But their blind faith in our venture, even just their support of Craig, is something I will never forget and am so incredibly grateful for.

The two of them gave us $25,000 in total. And it was enough. We were able to get started.

From this point on, we did not stop. We knew we'd been given the biggest lifeline of our lives, and while the pressure was off in terms of finding money, the pressure of getting Triangl to be a profitable business was most certainly on.

We placed our first order of swimwear, around 400 pieces, a few days after we received the money. With a few months of strategy planning behind us, our initial model was fairly simple. We had five prints for our release. All were digital prints, all were a triangle bikini and all were in the standard swimwear fabric, a nylon–spandex blend. We called the five different prints 'Moving to LA', 'Castles in the Air', 'Ten Mile

Stereo', 'Sherbet Bombs' and 'Paris Black' and they retailed for $79 a set. These original sets are still some of my favourites. We made a matching little bag in the same fabric for them to be stored in, and then packaged in another matte black box, meticulously sourced by Craig and custom made. Craig had an innate ability and almost obsession to source the highest quality fabrics and finishes at the cheapest cost. It was these product-focused touchpoints that helped set Triangl apart from day one.

He was forever looking for fabrics with the best four-way stretch and nicest hand feel.

Our original nylon/spandex was a standard fabric but our prints were all graphic screen prints, diligently positioned and applied to ensure they looked like they were of an exceptional quality. He was constantly sourcing the best version of neoprene once we launched our famous wetsuit styles, and, once the business grew, became particularly interested in finding recycled and sustainable options. The issue we always faced was that the sustainable and recycled fabrics never felt as good, never fitted as well, and never stretched fully in a way that meant the bikini would be as comfortable as possible when wearing it. With swimwear covering the intimate areas of your body, the way it felt when touching your skin was super important, and we could never match this feel with a sustainable option. Instead, once the business became profitable enough, we sourced fabrics from Europe such as Italian velvet and French jacquard from small family companies, some which had been operating for hundreds of years. While manufacturing always stayed in China, using these European fabric suppliers, and investing in slow fashion in this way – honouring the history of fabrics and fashion – felt special and brought us closer to the fashion heritage side of business, rather than a churn-and-burn fast-fashion company.

We had negotiated fantastic terms with our first manufacturer to produce our original nylon/spandex styles, which was a testament to not giving up when first told no, and were able to produce only a small number of styles per size so we could wait and see which sold best, and replace only what was selling. This lean model was another feather in the Triangl cap, and one which meant we were able to be super reactive to the swimwear the customer was most drawn to and therefore buying.

Our initial launch plan was to sell these bikinis in a few wholesale stores in Australia, primarily in Melbourne. We had made a trip home to Australia, a few months earlier, before our money ran out, to visit stores across our hometown with our samples and lock in some accounts. We had found a handful, and were able to use these connections when we launched to get our stock into stores. We used a consignment model, where only what was sold was paid for, which was a commitment-free model for the wholesaler, and one that allowed for us to take stock back, before they inevitably marked it down. Craig and I didn't like the classic retail markdown model, where a product's cost was slashed at repeated intervals during the year. We never wanted to mark down Triangl swimwear; we believed markdowns educated the customer to wait for such discounts and so devalued the brand.

Our launch plan also included selling swimwear to friends – introducing them to our brand and relying on word of mouth to grow the business over the summer. Both Craig and I had a fairly strong network in Melbourne in retail, and we relied on this as a tool for initial awareness of the brand.

Our online store was ready to go as well, and even though we both wanted that to be our main form of traffic and sales, we knew a business couldn't be launched online without some initial brand awareness, hence why we chose wholesale as well.

Our bikinis were ready in early December 2012. We decided I would return to Australia to manage our wholesale accounts and get some momentum happening around the brand.

I made it home a couple of weeks before Christmas and was thrilled to be there, especially with an actual real business to talk about. I flew home on the overnight flight, and even made it to my girlfriend's hen's party that same day I arrived. It wasn't by any means a glamorous moment though; I wasn't even able to afford to go to the actual hen's, only the first half of the day at her parents' house. I spent those first weeks hustling our initial collection from the boot of my mum's car and ended up doing this for three months. I stayed at my parents' house, in my old bedroom, which could have been a really triggering time, returning to your home you lived in as a child, as a dependant, but it wasn't. I felt like a different Erin back home this time, different to that young girl, that teenager even, who'd last lived there. I felt I was starting to access a part of me I had not before, and a certain ambition in me I hadn't known existed. I had control over a business, and, without Craig around, it felt really empowering. Craig often made me feel lesser than, not intentionally, but by just existing as he had more experience than me in all aspects of life. Without him, I was able to move forward with Triangl, while he stayed in Hong Kong focusing on sampling, creating, designing and producing. It was a perfect scenario, to be honest, and really allowed for Triangl to launch as it deserved to, with optimism, positivity and hope.

The launch had gone well. It felt like more of a relief than anything, to have a tangible brand, a real business to work on. Our wholesale accounts were going fine, and feedback was good. I was making a nice little bit of pocket money selling bikinis for cash from my car to friends over the summer who I knew were just supporting me, and who showed me how good it feels to ensure you truly support those around you. Those moments were so fulfilling for me, and I loved so much when a friend believed in me and bought a bikini.

In early January, we launched our website, our online store. As per trends at the time, we coined it an eboutique. It sounded higher end, and more luxurious, or even just more trustworthy. Both Craig and I were loath to ever do anything because it was what others did, and always wanted to make small changes to show our originality. This was one of those decisions, although I am sure we swiped it from somewhere else!

With the online store trading, and selling a bikini via the eboutique every few days, usually via a friend, or a friend of a friend, it all felt hopeful. I was using my personal Instagram at this point, sharing bits and pieces of my time in Melbourne, relating to the business. It was enough to garner some interest and look at Instagram in a really positive way. At this point, bloggers still had the lion's share of the online space. Whether it be on Tumblr, or their own personal page, bloggers were the ones everyone in fashion looked to. We were watching this all carefully at this stage, knowing we couldn't afford to pay the big bloggers (they were all monetising their personal brands on their blogs already), but wondering how and when we could tap into this powerful marketing tool.

It was a fairly nice time for the brand, and one which felt rather effortless and without too much pressure, as the space itself was in a sort of discovery mode with the overall online presence of fashion sales growing larger by the day. That being said, both Craig and I were wanting to scale up quickly. We had given up everything for this business and didn't want to settle for anything mediocre.

Throughout that first month, January 2013, Craig and I discussed how we both felt the brand needed a stronger point of difference. Nylon/spandex had been done before; it wasn't new. The price point was great; it was low, but the product wasn't exciting enough. We wanted something that people would talk about, that 'hook'. A few months before I left for Australia, Craig had sampled a bikini in wetsuit material, in neoprene. I remember fitting it in Hong Kong when it came, and we both immediately loved it. We did it in our shape of a triangle top and a hipster bikini bottom, and it just felt so good on. It was smooth and shapely, and I remember feeling sexy in it – an extremely rare occurrence for a very skinny 28-year-old woman. It looked airbrushed on the body, and just stayed there in place. We both knew using this material was a great idea, but we were both so busy launching our other styles that we didn't move on it.

It was during one discussion in January that Craig told me he'd sampled the neoprene in a few colours, and added a very simple black binding to the outline, to further enhance the shape and form of the style. He thought to do a small run of these neoprene styles, just to test them out. They were cheap to produce and the factory had agreed to a small run for us.

Why not? So we did. The intention was to sell them online only. Swimwear has very little hanger appeal, and this was a pain point of ours. Online felt easier too: fewer people to manage, fewer logistics to handle. We had a mannequin in Hong Kong that we shot all the samples on, and then edited them to put them online. I wrote all the copy and Craig supplied all the imagery.

Not only did the neoprene look different, it felt different. It had this appeal to it that was fresh and new, even though this fabric choice for bikinis had been around since the 1980s.

I feel it was largely because we were introducing it into the online space that it felt so different and new. It shot so amazingly well online as it lay flat to the body and so smooth. And when it made it into your hands, it felt just as good as it looked online.

The factor that made neoprene so special with how structured it was also required us to educate our customers that the bikinis had to be stored flat and could not be scrunched up in a drawer like other bikinis because they would inevitably crease and develop folds in the fabric. We learned this very much the hard way when our first order of neoprene bikinis were shipped to me in Australia. The box arrived, full to the brim with all 400 pairs. But they had not been packed carefully, and almost every single pair arrived with a very deep set of folds and creases. I immediately panicked. Moments like these were terrifying to a brand running on very little cashflow and could have signalled the collapse of the whole business. Before calling Craig and delivering the brand-killing news, I took out Mum's iron, turned the heat way up, and proceeded to try and iron out the folds, and it worked! The relief I felt in that moment was enormous and meant I was able to call Craig with the problem, followed quickly by my solution. I then had the entirely monotonous task of ironing every single bottom and top of every style, which took me four whole days and nights. Fortunately, my parents were in the final stages of moving house, and had packed up most of their furniture, so I turned their floors into a sea of colour-blocked neoprene bikini tops and bottoms. Once every pair was carefully packed back into their plastic sleeve, a huge enough task in itself, we were able to move forward with the launch of the neoprene 'Chloe' bikini.

We shot the bikinis on a girl in Perth, called Chloe. She was a girl I found on Instagram, and who immediately agreed to a shoot. In fact, we named the first bikini shape after her. Neither Craig nor I were there, but we trusted the beautiful WA beaches not to let us down. We paid a photographer in cash, and Chloe in bikinis, and the shoot was the first one we ever did.

I remember seeing those photos, and knowing we were on to something special. The combination of the white sand, blue water and a solid-colour structured bikini was incredible. It just somehow worked perfectly.

The images went on to the website and on to my Instagram account, which we soon changed from my name to Triangl Swimwear. It would take a few more years to be able to buy the Triangl handle from another user, but we also knew we needed Swimwear in the title initially anyway. We also used these images to email bloggers and girls on Instagram, as a marketing campaign as such. We went after all the popular bloggers, of course, but our tactic for the Instagram girls was to find alignment. I trawled Instagram seemingly all day, every day – finding girls who looked like they enjoyed being social by the pool or on the beach. I wasn't looking for the sexy women who wore bikinis to perhaps appeal to the opposite sex, but girls and women who liked looking good, and having fun with their girlfriends – they were the ones who were our best chance at liking a new swimwear brand. We also were offering them a bikini for free, *and* we never asked for anything in return. Genuinely nothing. I was honestly as interested in the feedback from them on the swimwear as I was in it being a marketing tool. This was my first foray into the act of nurturing my relationships, with both customers and influencers – basically anyone who was remotely interested in Triangl. In the beginning, it was with the girls who were to be our walking advertisements. My interactions with these girls and women were absolutely crucial. I was the voice of this new swimwear brand. It wasn't just product; in fact, product was the final piece of the puzzle. I wanted them to know I valued them and I valued their thoughts, so my communication with them was always thorough, authentic and super friendly. It helped that I genuinely loved connecting with these women, and I built strong and lasting relationships for years to come with these Triangl Girls, as they came to be known. Some I still talk to today, a good decade on, and I will always be indebted to them for all they did for Triangl, and for me personally. These initial points of connection and communication gave me back my life, my purpose. This was what I was here for; I was going to build Triangl through my word, my intent and my heart.

Sales were slow and steady using this method, but momentum felt strong and impactful. Not many brands were using Instagram as a marketing tool yet, but we had anticipated the power of this platform and it was starting to work for us. These women I had approached were 'tagging' our brand, and drawing attention to our Instagram page and our website. And, in turn, we were able to use their images on our page and tag them in return. It was a simple method, built off consistency and a level of quality control on the images themselves that were on our page. Aside from the interactions I had with these early influencers and my 'no post necessary' gifting strategy, we had a strict set of rules we applied to photos we reposted on our own page. We wanted those images to emulate a professional photoshoot as much as possible. We saw other brands by this stage posting anything and everything they received from an influencer, which in turn made their pages look scrappy and ugly. We wanted to set a tone for Triangl. A high-quality, beautiful offering across every single touchpoint possible. Product, packaging, website, customer care, emails, images. Our Instagram page always looked like an escape, a reminder of a holiday. And this sentiment, we felt, lent to purchasing a bikini as a moment of freedom, a moment of escapism. Every single thing was considered by us with this mindset, to result in the generation of a sale.

And it started working, enough to get me on a plane back to Hong Kong in early February, back to our little studio apartment.

My return to Hong Kong felt like a relief and a burden all at once. I had settled so easily back into my life in Melbourne over the summer, too easily, and my fear around Triangl being successful was muted by dinners with family, days at the beach (a benefit of an online focus meant my work was able to come with me anywhere), and a slower pace in general. Being back in Hong Kong meant a total, unwavering focus on Triangl. Craig and I had made no friends in the city, had built no relationships, so it was a solitary confinement as such, with a sole focus on building our brand to be better every day.

However, I was feeling good about our business; I'd found my place within Triangl and I was going for it. I monitored every single post we put on Instagram, diligently replying to and taking full care of every comment. I went even as far as to monitor every post that was made by someone else featuring Triangl, and commenting on any queries or questions that were on those posts too. At this point, we were selling three or four bikinis a week. But this was growing week on week. And this was the exciting part. We could see the growth, feel the growth. We knew what we were doing was slowly working, and alongside a product we truly believed in and were really proud of, it felt like we were on to a great overarching strategy for our business.

I found it so easy to talk about the neoprene. It felt exciting and challenging to be introducing this new fabrication to potential customers. The number of times I typed out 'the fabric sits flat on the body, creating a smoothing effect' would be a number I could not even begin to comprehend. I was hustling hard to ensure these potential customers felt so supported by this new brand that was doing something a little different in the swimwear space.

The bulk of interest was via Instagram, usually through another page where we had gifted a bikini to someone and then they found us. We were watching our site visitors regularly – I was perhaps a little obsessed with looking at it – and we had strong visit figures. But they'd drop off, usually without a purchase. I thought about this a lot. How could we keep them on the site and encourage them to purchase a bikini? We'd already launched the website with an impulse-purchasing mentality around it: keeping the offering small enough to be easy to digest, but enough to make them feel they needed something. I'd seen online stores where there were hundreds of styles and it was too overwhelming, but I'd also seen stores where there were only a few styles, which was too underwhelming. We chose to have fifteen styles displayed on our product page, displayed horizontally in rows of three. Craig and I wanted to give the customer enough choice without flooding them with options. It was something we were super protective of, and it often meant taking styles clean off the site, as we didn't mark anything down. We chose that loss of stock over the potential loss of sales through having too many styles, or by losing brand value by marking down our bikinis by having sales.

With our site aesthetics as clean as possible, I turned my focus to the customer-care side, and how I could mimic a physical store experience with a sales assistant at hand to guide the customer with sizing, styles and any pertinent questions.

I'd seen on a few big websites a live-chat option. It was usually reserved for the big companies, and I'd never seen it used for a fashion brand before, but it made perfect sense to add it to our site. I would manage it, as our influx of visitors wasn't anything too heavy to handle. We added Live Chat to the website, and directed our Instagram traffic there as much as possible to have a one-on-one, real-time conversation. This feature was the perfect addition to our new brand. I was not only able to chat to customers about all their queries, but it added a level of trust to the site. It was basically akin to a bricks-and-mortar store in that you had someone right there at your disposal, and it wasn't an empty portal, trying to steal your money, which was a real fear for people still at this time in the online space.

Live Chat was an absolute thrill to watch. It facilitated mainly sizing and shipping questions, and it truly assisted in so many direct sales. I took so much joy in these interactions with my customers. I was able to explain the origins of Triangl and the reason we had our brand, while also talking on specific styles and the features of them. I took such delight in explaining to customers how it was me on the Live Chat, the co-founder of the business, and I knew how important this was in building trust, loyalty and a word-of-mouth marketing model. I ensured these experiences were so uplifting, so positive, so lovely that these customers would tell their friends of this new brand selling great swimwear online.

I followed up on as many orders as possible, especially when women needed a bikini by a certain time, or where they were guessing sizes and perhaps thought they were getting it wrong. My mantra was to under-promise and over-deliver. It was the most rewarding experience to reach out via email to these customers and check in, to ensure their needs had been met. As humans, we all want to feel valued, heard, listened to, and these interactions in the early days of our business set the tone for Triangl to be a friendly, welcoming and supportive community. One built on authenticity, kindness and a lot of love. I have always held the firm belief that the customer is king, that they are number one. They were my boss, and I merely worked for them. Holding this strong core value was how these women trusted me, listened to me and ultimately bought from me, and I wholeheartedly believe these principles will always stand the test of time in a consumer-led business.

It was in these early months of 2013 that Craig's and my skill sets became completely separate and crystal clear. He designed and commercialised the bikinis in the way he brilliantly knew how, and I nurtured the sales process and marketing of the bikinis, from start to finish.

At this point in time, all sales were running through PayPal, and I had set up the app on my phone to 'ding' every time we received a sale. This notification on my phone felt like the greatest reward, and I recall the day I eventually had to turn it off due to too many dings, which made me feel quite sad that the initial growth chapter had moved on to a new stage. During those first few months those notifications were our biggest motivator; we often received them on a trip back from Sham Shui Po, a well-known fabric and trims area of Hong Kong, or while sourcing inspiration from the multiple high-end boutiques in the city, which you'd think would be fun for a fashion-obsessed girl, but most definitely wasn't when you couldn't ever afford to buy a single thing! There was such hope in these notifications, such promise; they became addictive and I kept them on 24/7, even feeling thrilled when hearing a ding at 3am. During this time, we experienced our first sell-out item. The black neoprene style was our highest selling item in these early months of 2013. Called New York Noir, it was the safest colour of the Chloe options, which made sense for a new brand that no one really knew they could trust yet. We had built in a model, based off the Zara model in terms of a quick sample-to-production-to-release timeline. Zara was at seven days, but being the global giant they were, we had no chance of such a short turnaround. However, we had worked out a way to get a bikini designed, sampled, produced and delivered in fourteen days. Considering the standard production timeline was closer to six months, we had a huge advantage in terms of keeping the offering lean, fashion and trend focused, and reactive to what was actually selling – we could place repeat orders only on the sizes and styles that were moving.

We somehow got caught out with New York Noir and we sold out of most sizes in the style unexpectedly. A well-known Instagram influencer had posted in the bikini, which resulted in a small influx of sales that sold us out. Taking the style offline felt like a real kick in the guts, but we kept it on a waitlist so we could notify the customers when the style would be back online.

A week or so later, the style returned to stock, we notified our customers and sold over one hundred pairs in a matter of an hour or two, resulting in so many of those little PayPal dings that it was completely surreal. Before this, our best day of sales had been around thirty pairs, so this showed us we had a customer database, and people interested and invested in the brand, and had first realised the desire for it was there.

The confidence this gave us propelled Craig and I and the brand forward, and we soon released a number of new styles, which only added to sales, growth and followers.

By April 2013, we were able to already pay back our friends the initial $25,000 in loans for the business, as well as an old $8000 debt Craig had with his ex-business partner from years ago, and a $30,000 debt I had built up over time with my dad, one which I never thought I would ever pay back. Triangl was cashflow positive from this point; we didn't take on any debt to grow the business and used money we had in the bank to take our next step, every time we were presented with one.

We were humming along nicely, though quickly outgrowing our fulfilment strategy, which was entirely reliant on Craig and me.

The number of orders a day had been steadily climbing, and we were selling thirty to fifty pairs a day by this stage. We were rapidly gaining traction, not only in terms of sales, but on Instagram too, with our followers. While no one very famous or well-known had been wearing the bikinis yet, we'd been making progress with our gifting strategy, and were getting seen on the Instagram pages of young women all over Australia. Nothing felt out-of-control busy yet, but our consistent growth in all areas of the business was apparent.

Every morning, I would print the orders, pick them from the storage boxes quite literally next to my bed, and then write out, by hand, every single address label. We were using Hong Kong Post to send orders out as it was the cheapest, and quite quick too. Our orders were predominantly going to Australia at this point, and the delivery time was around two or three days, which was very good. Craig and I had to make several trips every morning to the post office and stand in line to drop off the orders, using a giant plastic tub each. The romance of all these orders coming in wore off quickly when posting them started to take up almost our entire day, every day. We had no other option that we were aware of to streamline this process, other than to make the move and find a fulfilment warehouse. This was an exciting and big step forward, clearing up most of our day to focus on the growth of the brand, but a step that almost completely destroyed our business, not once but twice.

Chapter Four

Lean, Keen Triangl Machine

It felt thrilling, and surreal, to be discussing scaling the business in this capacity, only mere months after our first sale. I was quite enjoying our home/office/warehouse scenario but knew this wasn't exactly the best option if we wanted to continue to grow. When choosing a third-party fulfilment warehouse, we had a couple of options. To either pick a centre in Hong Kong, which at the time was rather expensive and involved the stock being sent from China to Hong Kong before being sent out. Or to choose a warehouse in China, which was a lot cheaper but admittedly a lot riskier. Hong Kong was definitely the more global, professional choice but as a small brand that was only a few months into a small level of success, we were still attracted to the cheaper option, even with its extra risks.

We found a facility in Shenzhen, China, extremely close to the border. This worked well in terms of mitigating the risk as I would be able to travel easily to the warehouse, and it felt like a good fit.

This wasn't my first experience with China, by any means. We'd found our factory not long after we first moved to Hong Kong. We did this by visiting the China Sourcing Fair specifically for swimwear and underwear, held in Hong Kong. A crucial piece of the puzzle in visiting this fair was finding the right manufacturer and factory. There were huge rooms of endless stalls with suppliers showcasing their samples, and so it was a bit of an art, not a science, to find the best stalls and keep your eyes peeled for samples from recognisable brands. No names were on the samples, of course, but if you were well versed in swimwear, as we were in those early days, you could pick which factories were manufacturing for which brands. Not that this was entirely helpful for us, as we weren't able to afford those suppliers anyway, although we most definitely tried.

I'd describe the experience as trying to find the right shop in a shopping centre. We were looking for nice fabrics, a professional stall setup (which usually mimicked the cleanliness and professionalism of the factory) and similar styles to those we wanted to make. Once we found a stall with a style we felt was aligned with what we were making, we'd stop and ask one of two questions: what is your MOQ (minimum order quantity)? The stallholder would be able to speak fairly good English, and if this question was answered satisfactorily for us (meaning the MOQ was low), we'd nod or say 'Okay, good', and ask the next question: 'Where are you based?' We needed to know the location, as a lot of the bigger factories were just south of Shanghai, which was too far away from Hong Kong because they would require a flight to visit, which we could not afford. We needed them to be from a factory near Guangzhou, another popular area for clothing, which meant we would be able to catch a train and a bus to the factory and back, which was much cheaper in those initial startup stages. The MOQ question was another quick rule-out option if they demanded anything over 500. We were not at all in the business of ordering thousands of units for reasons of both cashflow and our lean and reactive product-replacement method.

If our two questions were answered favourably, we would move in closer to the stall, which is when we'd be invited to sit down and often brought tea. We would be shown samples and fabrics, and, at this point, we would show a sample that we'd brought, which we'd already had made previously via a manufacturer Craig was using in his old job.

The manufacturers often sought sample orders to be placed then and there, which we did, after negotiating on the cost of the bikini. The sample cost was often higher than the cost of the bikini if produced; however, we always pushed to get the sample cost as low as possible, and this was also a good test to see how far the manufacturer was willing to negotiate.

We did this with four manufacturers at the fair, and ended up sampling with three.

This was a really strong push forward and, after arranging these sample orders, we returned home to wait for samples and then the negotiations to come.

Out of the three options, when samples did arrive (time of arrival being another important test to see how they would go fulfilling orders in time) there was a clear frontrunner. While the style wasn't exactly what we wanted, the quality was good. The stitching was neat, their understanding of what we wanted was fairly strong, and they were the quickest to send their sample to us.

We'd found our first factory. It was a minimum three and a half-hour trip from Hong Kong, consisting of a train ride to Shenzhen (which links Hong Kong to mainland China), which took an hour, crossing the border, which took anywhere from 30 minutes to 3 hours dependant on variables we could never work out, and a 2.5 hour bus to the factory, which was in a small town where basically no one spoke a word of English.

The first trip there was overwhelming to say the least. As Craig and I were tackling the factory process alone, compared to the more common (but more expensive!) path of using an agent, we were winging these trips and doing them completely on our own. We were staying in a hotel with a bed so uncomfortable it was like sleeping on the floor. We had made a few failed attempts at ordering food at little shopfronts, as we were trying to absorb ourselves in the culture of the city. However, after being presented with food we really couldn't eat, we ended up taking snacks up with us to our hotel room. For all future trips – which were usually no more than three days – we lived off nuts, dried fruit and biscuits.

We did eventually find our feet a little more, and even had a few favourite restaurants – one which served the most unbelievably delicious chocolate fondant dessert that is still, to this day, the best I have ever had. Of course, all this lack of good food played very well into my still ever-present anorexia. These factory trips were always rather stressful, as we usually were making them when we had an issue with a sample, a timeline of production or some other miscommunication between East and West. And with stress, naturally, came the control element, which meant I avoided food in order to have something I could control.

Walking the hour and a half journey to the factory from our hotel and back again, which we did every day to save money and also save the endless daily effort of trying to communicate when we couldn't speak the language to even arrange transport, I was able to process in real time, and think to myself that this slog we were putting ourselves through had to result in some level of success. We really were doing every single part of the setup and scaling of the business, in a way I had never heard of anyone doing before, and I was sure this would result in the universe acknowledging and returning the favour to us at some point.

~

With these early China trips under my belt, setting up the fulfilment warehouse in Shenzhen felt like a walk in the park. Practically all of our stock – a few thousand pairs of swimwear – was in our tiny apartment, so it was a straightforward task to get the stock out of there, given it was all in one place. Boxes upon boxes of styles, stacked floor to ceiling in every spare section possible.

In true 'lean startup' form (Craig had read *The Lean Startup* by Eric Ries and shared with me every single learning prior to Triangl launching), we wanted to get all this stock into the warehouse as easily as possible. This naturally meant doing it ourselves. But this wasn't just a simple case of putting the stock in a van and driving it to the warehouse; we needed to get the stock across the border, into China. Doing it ourselves meant avoiding the inevitable taxes applied by China for all goods entering the country. So, yes, we decided to illegally drive the stock across the border. A huge risk, but one we took so we could save a fair amount of money. We purchased some very cheap suitcases to house the bikinis in. Keeping the bikinis in the cardboard boxes would have raised the alarm for the border authorities, for sure, whereas we thought suitcases looked like we were going into China for a holiday. In hindsight, it was a stupid idea, but we were being incredibly optimistic that we could get away with it. We hired two vans with two drivers, and filled each one with three suitcases each. Craig was in one, and I was in the other one. We'd left a small amount of stock in Hong Kong as it didn't all fit, but we had packed the majority, which included our bestsellers and all our popular styles.

The way the border control worked with cars into China was that you lined up with either goods to declare or no goods to declare. Obviously, we went with the latter.

Regardless of whether we had items to declare or not, we had to drive through with the boot open, so a quick inspection could be made. I was one van behind Craig and watched them quickly check the boot and they seemed to be unperturbed with what they saw. In that moment, I felt relieved, and smug! I felt silly for having any doubts about our decision to sneak our stock through border control to avoid taxes given how easy it obviously was to get these cases across the border! Craig's van started to drive off, but they'd jumped the gun, as they hadn't actually been given the all-clear. The speed with which they started to drive off, combined with the fact the border control police hadn't yet closed the boot, was a clear signal that something was up, and the border control police came from everywhere to stop the van from going any further. As instantly as I'd felt the smugness came the absolute dread. I didn't even know what kind of implications were in place for breaking China's customs laws. In Australia, it was a fine and nothing more, and in Hong Kong I imagined a similar scenario. But we weren't in either place. We were in China. A country known for their extremely tough rules and regulations.

The gravity of what was about to take place hit hard, and as they checked the boot of my van, I knew we were absolutely screwed. My mind went immediately to jail time, and with Craig having been separated from me, I did not know what was about to happen. They'd taken Craig into their holding room, and I was left waiting outside, in my van. My suitcases had been confiscated as well, however for some reason, unbeknown to me, they left me sitting in the waiting room outside and had no interest in interrogating me. My mind was switching from sheer panic thinking he was being beaten, or taken to jail, or perhaps never to be seen again (dramatic, I know) to reasoning with myself that this was not a big deal, and he'd be let out after a little slap on the wrist, and that maybe, *maybe*, we'd get our stock back to at least return to Hong Kong with. After what felt like hours, and perhaps it was, Craig stepped outside of the room to tell me the stock was most likely being confiscated, as he was just told he could leave without being given anything at all to take with him. No paperwork, nothing. This did feel like a huge relief, to be honest, after all the awful scenarios my mind had been conjuring up in Craig's absence.

Craig had been in the holding room pleading for the stock to be returned, but not even being told anything in English, and not having anyone to contact for confirmation of what was going on. In fact, we never were told anything else afterwards, and we did wait for something more to come of it; perhaps a fine, or a court date, or something – anything! But we simply lost all our stock and the suitcases, and were never to hear of it again.

My initial relief over the fact Craig wasn't being taken off to a Chinese jail fell away rather quickly at the sobering thought that we'd just lost all our swimwear. We didn't have much time to sit and sulk though; Craig left that very next day to go to our factory and push additional orders through to replace the confiscated stock, while I stayed in Hong Kong to email everyone who'd ordered a bikini and was about to have a slightly longer than expected wait. Fortunately, though, we had been topping up our stock holdings in preparation for the warehouse move anyway and were able to rush a few smaller orders through to cover it, no doubt due to Craig's perseverance at the factory.

A few days later I was at the fulfilment warehouse to teach the team about how to process and pack the orders. Stock had started already arriving, which was a huge relief and it felt like we were going to get away with our border crossing debacle without any real hardship.

I was staying in a hotel near the warehouse, and, as we were in Shenzhen, it all felt very Western, and the hotel – a brand-new one at that – was decent. It was good to be based somewhere that didn't feel completely foreign to me because although I was absolutely fascinated by Chinese culture and history, it was still difficult for me to understand and feel comfortable with an entirely different way of living from what I was accustomed to. As much as I appreciated that East and West have very different ideologies, it was at times unbelievably frustrating and often dumbfounding to be presented with the challenges pertaining to our different belief systems, especially when it came to business dealings. At this point in the development of our business we found the challenges to be nothing more than minor inconveniences, but they were soon to become far more major.

I spent these initial handover days with the Chinese manager of the Shenzhen warehouse facility, Jackson, unpacking every bikini style and setting them up in their respective sections myself, to ensure packing systems were followed to the letter. We had a fairly easy but specific packing system, as bikinis were sold as sets, but with the option to choose a different top and bottom size – so both pieces had to be picked separately and were listed separately on the order sheet. I spent 15- to 16-hour days at the warehouse in this first week, meticulously labelling every single section and going over the process step by step with Jackson and the other members of the team. I survived on cans of Fanta and packets of biscuits as the warehouse was on the outskirts of Shenzhen, in a new industrial area, where no food outlets were nearby, nor was there anything near the hotel.

No one in the team except Jackson understood English, or at least I thought he did. He and I went over an example of picking an order, numerous times, and he would enthusiastically nod in agreement, each time, as I carefully explained everything. We did have a Chinese local, Cathy, who spoke English and was working with us on occasion as a translator when we needed to discuss business with anyone in Mandarin or Cantonese. Cathy usually met us in China to assist with these interactions, but she was with Craig at the factory, where no one spoke a word of English either, and he required her to translate constantly to ensure our bikinis were being made correctly and new samples were moving along quickly – as new arrivals were crucial to us at that stage, and already forming a large part of our strategy.

I remember wishing so badly that I could speak more than a few words of Cantonese and Mandarin, which I'd cobbled together over the last nine months. Once we realised how important it was to be able to speak and understand these languages, we were already stretched to our absolute limit of having enough hours in the day for Triangl, and it wasn't an option to take on learning two new languages as well.

I spent a full week at the warehouse, ensuring the processes were set out in the same steps as we had been doing ourselves in Hong Kong. I wanted customers to not even know there had been a changeover of the fulfilment process, and it made me feel anxious at the thought that even one customer might feel let down.

This was a common theme during our growth years, of having to let go of certain duties so we could focus on the more 'important' tasks, but it always filled me with dread, as it felt like I was losing connection with the most important parts of Triangl, and the most important parts of me. I'd found my place connecting to the customer, and didn't like losing it at any point along the way.

Once the week was up, I left Shenzhen and made my way to Jiangmen to urgently fit samples that needed my attention. I was the fit model, or muse – as my ego wants to write – for all the Triangl styles. I fitted every bikini for the first three years, and Craig and I formed quite the formidable team in terms of ensuring every bikini looked and felt exactly as we wanted it to. This, however, was quite an ongoing trigger for me during these first few years as there was pressure on me to maintain a certain shape, and look the same. I naturally obsessed over staying 'sample size', and being as small as possible.

Our fittings were often in our apartment in Hong Kong, or they would be in the factory, in front of everyone. It was never an issue for me, though. Being the fit model played in nicely to my dissociative ways, when I reflect on it. In my head, I was just a commodity in the business, not anyone actually driving or running or managing it. These were the thoughts I'd often have in my head when fitting samples. I was just the model and Craig was the one in charge.

We'd often have to fit samples in the factory, submitting changes, and then wait for the new samples to be made, often in the same day, and then fit again. We'd repeat this process until the fit and style were perfect, and then we'd place the order. It was the most unglamorous way to work on our swimwear, but the most efficient – it was how we were able to turn product releases around so quickly.

This particular trip lasted for around three days, and we then returned to Hong Kong, to our now fairly empty apartment, which felt a bit sad as it was the end of an era for us to see almost no stock in there. Our living space was now only a standard home office rather than a warehouse as well.

In my busyness since leaving Shenzhen, coupled with some level of comfort in knowing I'd set up the fulfilment warehouse with as much clarity over the picking and packing process as possible, I'd not been in touch with Jackson and the team (via Cathy to translate) for a couple of days, and very naively assumed this meant all was running smoothly.

It was when I received an email from a customer, telling me they'd received the wrong top and bottom, and not just in terms of sizes but a different coloured top and bottom, that I immediately felt something was very wrong. I knew in my gut, at that moment, that this wasn't going to be the only issue. It was suddenly so obviously clear, that the fulfilment warehouse, full of non-English speakers, didn't actually know what to do at all and were most likely guessing orders. A swift phone call to Jackson also made it crystal clear to me that he couldn't understand what we were saying at all. It was one of those earth-shattering moments, where I realised I'd been running on hope and optimism and ignoring what was actually going on in front of me.

Both Craig and I packed a bag within ten minutes, which we were very used to doing when working with and in China, and jumped on the train to Shenzhen, where we walked into the warehouse to my worst nightmare becoming a reality.

Jackson, for the first time, was not his usual happy self, and was largely avoiding talking to us at all. We were waiting for Cathy, our translator, to come down from her home in mainland China, but we'd seen enough to know before even talking that things were bad.

The system I had set up was completely non-existent. Our packing slips were in numerous locations all over the warehouse, with no markers as to whether they had been fulfilled or were brand-new orders. There was no record anywhere of what had been sent out already, and no one to tell us a single thing about it.

Cathy arriving and having some urgent discussions with the team only proved what we already knew – the system I had set up was not being followed, and the so-called system they were following wasn't even able to be explained by anyone at all in the warehouse.

With no time to waste on pointing the finger of blame at anyone, we proceeded to start again.

I was absolutely responsible for what happened, and took full accountability, but there wasn't any time to wallow in feeling bad about myself; I went straight into action mode, setting up the system again, which was basically the same as the first system I had demonstrated, the only difference being we had Cathy to translate for us, and actually explain in Mandarin what needed to be done.

These moments were always uplifting, moments that happened time and time again when language was a barrier, when you had a third party to bridge the gap and you realised you were on the same page, fighting the same fight. The workers were diligent, they were quick, they wanted to do their job well, but they didn't even know what they were supposed to do because they'd basically not been told. (It was not a huge surprise, and admittedly somewhat of a confirmation that I wasn't a complete idiot, when Jackson wasn't at the warehouse on our next visit because he'd been moved along.)

Now we had to attempt again to make the picking and packing process as straightforward for the workers as possible. I managed which orders had been fulfilled, which orders hadn't been, and which orders had been fulfilled incorrectly over the past two weeks. We stayed for one night in

Shenzhen and returned to the warehouse the next day to find a smooth process now operating. The workers took to it quickly, and we were able to return home to Hong Kong, to face what turned out to be the toughest weeks of my entire working life.

I had taken home all the old orders I found in the warehouse, stacks of them, with the hope I would be able to work out what had been sent and what hadn't. But those stacks of papers were completely useless and served only as reminders that we'd fucked up on a huge number of orders. I had to make the assumption that the orders were never fulfilled in full from the first day we had started using that warehouse.

It was a logistical nightmare, and one made worse by the fact I knew I was letting down customers who were waiting for their order, but I didn't even know which customers were missing orders!

My options felt grim. One was to email everyone who'd placed orders over those two weeks, and let them know there'd been a processing error and that their order was going to be maybe wrong, or not even arrive at all. This was risky, though, because at this stage we didn't know if maybe a lot of the orders had been sent correctly and that we just had no record of it. I didn't want to admit a failing like this at a relatively early stage in our business. I thought it would cause the customer to lose trust in us, and as trust was the absolute forefront of my every interaction with my customers, I just felt this wasn't the right move. Another option was to send every order out again, as if none had been sent. This was two weeks of orders, so around maybe 1000 bikinis. No small number for a small business. Sure, we were growing, but this was still a hard pill to swallow. With that financial loss at stake, we chose not to do this either.

In the end, I basically had to be a sitting duck and wait for customers to contact me, whether that was to inform me of an incorrect bikini arriving or to chase the order and query why it hadn't arrived yet (another of Triangl's benchmarks was our 'super-fast' shipping, and we'd drilled this into our customers' expectations of us, so they did indeed chase when it took more than a handful of days). It was at that point that I explained what had happened, and immediately sent a replacement or fulfilled the order. The benefit of this was that I was able to maintain the personal connection and communication, which was much better than had I sent out a bulk email. Making the customer feel valued was an important factor to focus on as a priority in a consumer-led business.

I worked quite literally twenty-hour days during this process. The additional nurturing it took to overcome the grievances customers had was exhausting, and I gave those negatively impacted customers everything I had to ensure they didn't write us off after this experience. Perhaps I was being overly cautious, but I always believed in the flow of energy through good experiences, and I especially had experienced the power in being able to turn a negative experience into a positive one. So, in a way, I actually saw this drama as an absolutely huge opportunity for building loyalty and trust through an experience that may have been seen as causing the opposite.

I was so invested in this process, and also so unbelievably stressed at the thought of losing a customer because of our initial difficulties with the warehouse, that even Craig took it upon himself to insist I take a night off and go and get a drink just up the road from our apartment. I must have been a shell of a human at this point for Craig, a workaholic who absolutely hated alcohol by this point, to insist I go and get a drink with him. Craig's relationship with alcohol had really soured in the year since we'd been in Hong Kong, to the point where he rarely had a drink and very much loathed if I ever did. It had stemmed from those early months when we'd just moved to the city, and I would drink to excess and then we would have huge fights. They were really heated arguments and they would always blow up so much more aggressively due to alcohol. We'd be having a lovely night until he would say or do something that I took issue with, and I would react so strongly, and then the pattern would unfold, as it always did, where we'd return home to our apartment to yell and scream obscenities at each other. One particular time, I threw a book at him as hard as I could, hitting him directly in the stomach, and another time, he pulled my engagement ring off my finger and threw it out the window of our fourth-floor apartment. (By some miracle, it had landed on an awning, and we'd seen it sparkling in the moonlight and he was able to climb a wall and get it.) These fights were always met with the same regret and soft words spoken the next morning, but they were toxic, and so badly fuelled by alcohol that it was no wonder Craig now resisted the idea of either of us drinking at all.

That night out where he insisted we get a cocktail lasted for only about an hour because all I could think about was getting back to my bed (where I was working from to save time each day and night) and getting back to saving Triangl and the sentiment of trust, reliability and exceeding customer expectations we had built around the brand.

Slowly, the emails became fewer and fewer, and I felt satisfied that we'd avoided a disaster. A disaster not in the sense of anything logical, but in terms of the good energy the business had around it. There was a 'feeling' around the business by this point. Craig and I never discussed it, I imagine for fear of it then not eventuating, but we could both feel it. We were on to something so big here, and I felt in my core that it was reliant on this momentum, this energy, this push of good feelings. It drove us to keep going, and do absolutely nothing other than work.

The few months after this, Craig and I only occasionally were in Hong Kong at the same time. He was camped out at the factory in Jiangmen, making samples, ensuring production was moving forward quickly, and maintaining the level of quality we were really becoming quickly known for. I was travelling to and from the warehouse in Shenzhen almost every single day to ensure operations were running smoothly.

I'd wake up in Hong Kong and work for a few hours from bed. Then I'd rush down to the MTR train station, and, knowing it would be all I was going to eat all day, grab a club salad from Pret A Manger. Craig and I lived off Pret as soon as we had a little more money to spend on food, and happily continued the tradition of eating there several days a week in the years to come. The simplicity of a ready-to-purchase salad was one we were always drawn to. Those minutes we saved preparing our own food, or even having something prepared for us at a nicer salad bar, added up over the years. These small decisions are often some of the ones that shape every part of your business approach.

With salad in hand, I'd take the one-hour train to the border, furiously typing away on my laptop and my phone, aware of the countdown that was on, before my access to Instagram disappeared as I approached China. It usually stopped just before I crossed the border, which was why I was doing so many trips back and forth. It would have been far easier to stay in Shenzhen, but I had no access to any social media there and we were reliant on my being able to maintain the gifting process to people we perceived as influencers, and the curation of our business page, and the nurturing of our customers.

Crossing the border back to Hong Kong was sometimes very quick and sometimes took hours. It was the biggest relief to see no queues and know I'd be able to make it back home before midnight. But many days, even though I'd only needed to spend an hour or two at Shenzhen to ensure orders were being fulfilled, I'd not be back home in Hong Kong until close to midnight due to the customs queues. The beauty of Hong Kong, though, was that I'd be coming back into a vibrant, pulsing city, especially near where we lived. Midnight, on any day of the week, was still incredibly busy, with people at bars, people leaving work, just people everywhere. I never felt alone, I never felt scared or vulnerable and I never felt like I was working that much harder than anyone else.

Despite all my best efforts and management, it didn't take long for the fulfilment warehouse in China to become an unsustainable model. Orders were taking longer, not due to the warehouse itself but because of China customs, who held almost all our orders trying to leave the country for days. Knowing this was a battle we would never win, or even try to win, we moved fulfilment to a third-party warehouse in Hong Kong. We needed to pay a fair bit more, but, for the ease of the whole process, it felt like an absolute no-brainer of a choice. The Hong Kong warehouse also assisted in taking care of getting stock from the fulfilment warehouse we'd used in Shenzhen, which ended up being quite the intimidating and confronting process, which I was very thankfully shielded from. We learned there were no friendly exits when it came to doing business in China, and the staff of our Hong Kong warehouse knew this all too well, and advised I stay well out of it.

Compared to the China warehouse, the one in Hong Kong was absolutely seamless in all processes. They took care of everything, and it was a decision that really took away all stress and responsibility from us, which was well worth the extra dollars it cost us.

With fulfilment taken off the list of major items we needed to sort out, we breathed a huge sigh of relief, glad we were going to be able to move into a slightly more enjoyable phase of the business and focus on the more exciting and visionary parts of developing Triangl into a trusted swimwear brand. One that not only we, but also our customers, would be passionate about.

Chapter Five

Taking Stock

I remember when Craig got the phone call, from an acquaintance who was also living in Hong Kong and manufacturing out of our same factory. He told Craig he saw something while he was in the factory, and he had taken some photos he wanted to show us. I had no idea what to expect; my mind went to something being ethically wrong, that he'd uncovered some kind of sweatshop situation. We had spent a lot of time in this factory and were happy enough with the conditions. They weren't the conditions I'd expect in Australia, but they seemed okay compared to what I'd read about during my obsessive discovery phase into the Chinese factory way of life. However, they always knew of our impending arrival before we visited, so I thought that perhaps they'd been hiding terrible conditions or children working or something of this nature.

Fortunately, what they were hiding wasn't anything like this, but what it was had a direct and menacing impact on our business. It was something neither Craig nor I had ever imagined possible but it was something, once we discovered it, that we kind of almost felt silly we hadn't prepared ourselves for.

This was often the way when dealing with China and sometimes even Hong Kong.

The way business was conducted and operated was just so different to our Western way of doing things. Things we assumed would be just a given, such as loyalty or transparency, were not at all this way, and, to this day, I still look back on some of the issues we faced with our suppliers in China and wonder if it was just a language barrier causing communication breakdown and cultural confusion, or if some the people we did business with were far more calculated in their approach and dealings than they ever let on.

I would have been surprised if what was shown to us in the photos was something unethical happening. We were across all that went on in that factory in terms of who supplied what and where it came from. We had met with every supplier personally, and visited their factories when it was possible. Zips, boxes, fabric, mould cups, the list goes on. We did this because we wanted to ensure every supplier took our orders seriously and gave us the best quality. We felt really comfortable with everyone we were working with, and had relationships that allowed us to directly communicate, albeit through a translator most of the time, with all suppliers when and if we needed to.

So, when I first saw that the photos were of our bikinis in tubs besides the machinists – sewed, finished products – I thought perhaps it just meant they were letting finished bikinis sit unpackaged for too long, a minor issue, if one at all really. But upon closer inspection, we noticed the sew-in labels, where our brand name should have been on the tag. These labels didn't say 'TRIANGL', but instead said 'BRAKINIS'.

We'd invented the word 'brakini' earlier in the year, when we launched our second-ever style, which was a fixed triangle shape and one we likened to more of a bra style, hence the name 'brakini', a play on the words 'bra' and 'bikini'. It was only a fun name, nothing too serious, just an easy way to explain the difference between our original triangle halter-neck style and this one. However, seeing the name sewn onto what appeared to be our bikinis felt very serious, and we immediately knew what was going on. They were passing off our brand, and using our exact fabric, exact trims, exact sewing technique to make extra bikinis for themselves with their name on them instead of ours. This kind of practice within factories wasn't unheard of, but we assumed, using the small factory we had found and getting to know everyone within that factory quite well, that it was not even possible that they would take our styles and pass them off as their own. It never even entered our minds, so seeing this physical proof was completely devastating.

Craig immediately left for China to spring a visit on them and hopefully catch them in the act. He let only Cathy know that he was coming and to arrange a car at the Shenzhen border to take him straight to Jiangmen. I needed to stay in Hong Kong to continue working because the factory in China never had working internet, and, of course, both Facebook and Instagram were banned in China, so I was unable to run my whole part of the business whenever I was in China. I was somewhat relieved not to accompany him to China because I was able to manage my work time much more efficiently in Hong Kong and I also found working alone a much nicer experience than when Craig was around. While our separate skill sets were the perfect combination for Triangl, they worked against us when it came to our personal relationship, and conflict was a regular occurrence. I'd built such resentment towards Craig by this stage, and honestly felt like I was only able to breathe when he left for China or on any kind of trip where I was left to my own devices. When I look back on this time, I realise it was likely nothing at all to do with Craig and more my own desire to be alone with my chaotic thoughts, so I could obsess over how I looked and what I ate or didn't eat, without him picking up on my disordered thinking and obsessive thoughts. Projecting my resentment at myself onto him came very naturally, and was much easier to do than to have to face my own issues. However, Craig leaving for this specific trip, while providing a small moment of relief to be alone once again, was largely overshadowed by the fear of what he was about to walk into at the factory.

When he did arrive, a number of hours later, he was unable to find any proof of them passing off our products, which surprised us both as we'd assumed he'd walk into something more obvious – or perhaps we were just hoping for that to happen. He spoke to the factory owner and showed her the photos, which she flat out denied as being true. Which was a bizarre situation to be in as the proof was right in front of her, but, sure enough, she shook her head and told Craig they weren't our bikinis. In fact, all she kept saying was 'no', shaking her head with defiant insistence.

Her response didn't make any difference to us, as once we'd seen the irrefutable evidence in the photos, we'd made the decision to part ways with the factory and go to another manufacturer.

Fortunately, we had already been sampling with another, better, cleaner, bigger factory, reason being that we had been discussing another gap we saw in the market, which was (and I believe still is!) underwear. This new factory, in Heyuan, China, predominantly made underwear, but they also did swimwear, and so were sampling already both some new underwear styles and our current swim styles.

Craig returned to his hotel in China that evening and proceeded to not only confirm with this new factory that we were going to move forward with them, urgently, but also – this time without involving Cathy in his plans – arranged a driver and a truck to turn up at the current factory, unannounced, and fill it with all our finished styles, incomplete bikinis, fabrics, trims – the whole lot.

After a relatively sleepless night for both of us, Craig called me on the way to the factory. I felt so incredibly useless in Hong Kong, but also knew it was necessary to be there, and that I would not have been able to offer anything of practical use to anyone on the ground in China.

Craig kept me on the phone the whole time, so I heard everything in real-time. The gates to the factory were open, as they usually were during the day, and Craig and the driver were able to drive the truck right in. I heard Craig explain calmly that he was at the factory to take our stock back, which was fair enough as we had paid for and supplied every single thing for our swimwear at that factory ourselves. We knew they would be blindsided by what was happening and show frustration, and perhaps we knew what was going to inevitably happen, but we were only applying best-case scenario thinking to this situation in explaining that we didn't want any drama, just to take back our stock and supplies.

Craig and the driver (who we'd paid very well in cash) started to take stock out of the factory and load it into the truck, without any real protest from any factory staff (it was early, and the owner and manager weren't in yet). They were making great progress, enough for Craig to tell me he'd call me back with an update later. I was wary but feeling optimistic that we may get out of this scenario largely unaffected. Not even thirty minutes later, Craig called back and I knew immediately that things had taken a turn for the worse. 'They've closed the gates and locked us in,' he told me, and my stomach dropped. I realised Craig was in a stand-off situation, in China, a country known for not taking kindly to Westerners who come and disrupt their way of living. I could hear the adrenaline in his voice, and this was alarming to me as I knew Craig had a fiery temper when pushed too far. And I could hear how far he was being pushed. He told me they'd brought 'heavies' to the factory to stand at the gates and at the back of the truck, effectively stopping any movement by Craig at all. I could hear him talking emphatically to the manager and the heavies, telling them that this was our stock, that we owned it so were allowed to take it, but there was no English being spoken from their side, and of course Cathy wasn't there or anyone else who could translate. Craig was in an incredibly frightening predicament, and while it was a terrifying prospect to lose all of our stock, I was far more frightened in that moment for Craig's life. I knew the situation was on the precipice of turning physical, and that meant nothing but pure danger. I wanted to help find a solution, get someone on the phone to translate, to explain why we just wanted our stock back, because none of this was even our doing to get to this point, but I also didn't dare get off the phone to Craig as I was fearful it may be the last time I would ever talk to him. I started pleading with him, repeatedly, to get out of there, to just leave. That we would work out how to get new stock, that he could be arrested if he stayed or, worse, killed. The mere act of voicing these concerns out loud sent me into a hysterical, hopeless state. The phone chose in that moment to go dead. Of all the moments, it was then!

I tried to call back and couldn't connect. I just felt numb, and couldn't entertain any other thoughts; I just kept trying to call, over and over again. When I finally got through, I could hear movement in the background, and I could tell by his breathing that he was walking, fast. He had left the factory, via the factory floor, through the front, and was on the street.

Standing at 193 centimetres, he was fortunately a fairly intimidating-looking person, and no one stopped him as he left, which made sense, but in that heated moment, who knew what was possible? He proceeded to tell me he'd pushed one of the heavies, and feeling the rage rise within his body, knew he was about to get into serious trouble and got out of there straight after, leaving the truck and all our stock. The driver of the truck was long gone by this stage, and Craig had no other option but to leave by foot. He came straight home to Hong Kong, and we strategised our next moves. We had stock in our warehouse, not a ridiculous amount, but it was enough. We placed fabric orders with our supplier, which was usually a very quick turnaround, and while trims took longer, we very fortunately had supplied the new factory with trims to make the initial samples and it was enough to sustain the orders until the replacement order arrived.

We never attempted to take our stock back, nor deal with our former factory directly ever again. We moved forward, with our new factory, which was a blessing in disguise, as they were able to execute a volume of orders that we were soon going to need.

~

While we'd solved the problem of finding a new manufacturer, and escaping without too much, or really any, negative impact on bikini sales, we were about to be faced with a far greater and long-lasting problem: the realisation we had our first copy-cat brand, Brakini, and that the issue was worse than we had imagined.

We soon found out that our translator, Cathy, was in on the whole thing, which was the absolute biggest kick in the guts, as we had really relied on her and trusted her implicitly. It felt like the ultimate betrayal.

We also found out that Brakini had mimicked our entire website, with names, styles, images and, of course, the product, and had hired an English-speaking team to copy our strategy with gifting. All their knowledge had clearly come from Cathy, who knew every single part of our business.

The biggest kicker, though, and one which introduced us to the wildly expensive and time-consuming world of registrations and trademarks, was that they had filed an application for not only the name 'Brakinis' in China but, more alarmingly, for TRIANGL. They were coming for us, and while we knew, as a Western brand, selling to the Western world, that we had the upper hand, it felt violating to witness this blatant and direct form of imitation.

We had no choice but to begin filing applications for trademarks and registrations in all jurisdictions across the world to beat this so-called brand to it. We started with our biggest markets, naturally, Australia, the USA, UK and Europe, but also Asia now felt necessary, and other locations that were renowned for their copy-cat brands. For example, in Indonesia, a copy-cat brand successfully registered the trademark for Polo Ralph Lauren before the original company did, and were allowed to trade under that name, without repercussions, throughout Indonesia, and, specifically, Bali, a city very often visited by international tourists, looking to shop on their holiday.

We didn't want the same to happen to us, and, being a very fast-growing brand, we had to embark on the very costly and time-consuming journey to ensure our brand was protected as much as possible.

I like to say that the key to beating copy-cats is innovation, and we were able to fairly quickly move past Brakinis with our styles, and, without our bikinis to steal directly, they were unable to keep up with what we were doing and they soon faded into oblivion.

This was only the start of the copy-cat era, and one we found to become fairly relentless as we continued to grow at the rate we were.

For some reason, we used to discover these copy-cats late at night, usually just before our already late bedtime. And they then kept us up for hours more, dissecting who was copying our brand this time. In Australia, it was pretty widespread by many small and mid-sized businesses, and we were copied constantly. It was frustrating, but with our main market in the US by this point, the Australian copy-cats felt more like a minor aggravation than anything else. We sometimes sent cease-and-desist letters, and these would sometimes work, but more often than not they didn't. It is actually very hard to prove a brand has copied you, due to very loose laws around what you can register in terms of designs.

We found this out when we were alerted to bikinis popping up on the Victoria's Secret website looking very much like ours. They were absolute dead ringers. And in our biggest market, to have one of the biggest players release bikinis that looked just like ours made us absolutely furious.

We wanted to go hard on this one, and fight Victoria's Secret. They were known in the space for this kind of behaviour, and we didn't want to take it lying down. We initiated lawyers and started the process, ambitiously and directly. We sent a letter and it was swiftly met with the most comprehensive reply, featuring examples of vintage styles, where they had referenced their bikinis and that they in no way had ever even seen our small brand before.

We knew this was an absolute load of BS, but they knew how to play the legal game and they knew how to play us. Our lawyer told us it was going to most likely cost over a million dollars to push on with the argument, and we didn't want to spend the money and, more importantly, the time fighting a seemingly unwinnable fight, so we dropped it.

It also was something the industry did, constantly reference other brands in the same category to see who was doing what, and well. I won't pretend we didn't do it; of course we did. But we did it largely with integrity and ensured we were as original as possible.

This was harder in the swimwear space, with little fabric to work with, but we made it a priority to always try our best to innovate. We adopted this mentality going forward as much as we could. There will always be copy-cats; it's how the industry works. A focus on innovation is what will propel a brand forward, and to innovate takes dedication and commitment, and we knew this meant we had to stop looking at those brands chasing our tails and focus on future fabrics and future designs.

After our two almost consecutive logistical dramas in China, we decided to take a holiday in September 2013 and joined one of Craig's best friends Simon, and his wife, Lucinda, on a trip to New York.

While all trips always resulted in maintaining a level of work, as was inevitable when having your own business, this trip was primarily for fun.

Being my first-ever visit to New York, I was unbelievably excited. It was also my first-ever business-class flight, so it's no surprise I did not sleep a wink for the entire seventeen-hour flight because I wanted to relish every moment. We flew through Taiwan on our way and arrived in New York around midnight. Our hotel was in NoHo and had a distant view of the Chrysler Building. New York is truly the only city I have ever visited in my life that not only matched my lofty expectations but exceeded them at every single point. It was the most exhilarating two weeks of my life, a holiday that I promised myself, on arrival into the city, wasn't going to be bound by my disordered eating, which by then was purely a control mechanism that was manageable enough but still kept me well below a healthy weight. More honestly, it was keeping my mind in a constant state of being 'busy', and was just so exhausting when my mind was already so full of all things Triangl.

I spent two weeks in New York eating everything I wanted to, which consisted of an almost daily breakfast sandwich at Café Gitane, red velvet cakes from Little Cupcake Bakeshop that were almost too sweet to stomach, and endless fries and other assorted carbohydrates. I spent this trip allowing my mind to feel free of restrictive eating. It was the best city to do this in, a city that allowed for freedom of expression, for you to be whoever you wanted to be, with no judgement.

We rode bikes every day, from Central Park, downtown and back up again, shopping and snacking every chance we got. Pretzels and hot dogs between meals, and American chocolate I'd never had before and needed to try. We went to Radio City Hall to watch a favourite band of mine, The xx, play, watched the Mets play baseball and drank sugary margaritas whenever we saw fit (which was a lot).

Being with our friends meant we had to switch off from Triangl, and our work – and it was a break I felt I needed, and thoroughly enjoyed.

Craig and I were somewhat tumultuous during this time. Any time away from Triangl caused Craig to feel some level of discomfort and uneasiness, in contrast to my complete enjoyment over being able to switch off even a little. This, plus excessive alcohol in the mix, led to some fiery arguments. As was the norm with Craig and me, our next day was always met with optimism over the future, perhaps because we both knew a relationship breakdown was far more involved than two people, thanks to our baby, Triangl.

I put on five kilos in this short period, which was a lot, and naturally sent me into a spiral of shame. Due to my fast metabolism, the weight came off very quickly, but it was more that as soon as I acknowledged the weight gain my self-loathing returned at a rapid pace, and the punishment I inflicted on my body in the weeks to follow took me right to my natural state which was a toxic relationship between my mind and my body.

~

On our return to Hong Kong, and after lugging our suitcases up our four flights of stairs, we decided it was time to leave our first home in Hong Kong and take up residence elsewhere.

We were travelling a lot, and planned for even more travel in the next year, so we needed a place that was going to suit our constant comings and goings and require very little upkeep. This was very simple to find, given the population of Hong Kong was so transient, and we headed straight to the Four Seasons the next day, a traditional and beautifully classic five-star hotel on Victoria Harbour, situated right next to the IFC Mall, one of Hong Kong's best shopping malls. The Four Seasons had a smaller building right next door, Four Seasons Place, and they had a one-bedroom harbour view apartment available, fully furnished, cleaned every day (bar Sundays), and a much-needed indulgence for Craig and me in our busy lives.

This was a big move for us, a massive commitment, and one that felt good because it was an acknowledgement of our success so far.

We moved in the next day; however, we only enjoyed the apartment for a couple of weeks, deciding not long after moving to head back somewhat home to Australia, to spend a few months working not from Melbourne, but rather a place on Bondi Beach, and making the most of an Aussie summer.

The allure of working from 'wherever we wanted' was formed here, and the Triangl tagline 'summer never ends' became one we embodied from this decision onwards.

The choice between a Hong Kong winter and an Australian summer felt like a no-brainer, so we took our laptops – which was where our business lived – and kissed HK goodbye for a few months.

Chapter Six

Triangl Girls

Dear (name),

I'm Erin Deering, founder of Triangl Swimwear, and I wanted to get in touch quickly.

I love your page, and your cute photos in (place to be inserted) – we'd love to send you a gift – with no obligation to post or share! We just want to get you in Triangl!

Please let me know your favourite style and sizes, with your best postal address, and I'll send a pair out to you straight away!

Kindest,
Erin xx

This was the email I sent over and over and over and over again.

The Triangl Gifting Program, as it became known, was our only marketing strategy. It was born out of total necessity, but fit our brand ethos perfectly: our desire to be an approachable brand. A brand that felt like a friend, or a brand that wanted to be your friend. Craig and I both had a severe distaste for 'cool' fashion brands. Brands that acted like they were cooler than you, and adopted a strategy of unfriendly, 'cool' communication.

Perhaps it worked sometimes in stores (or perhaps customers were just used to it), but online, it felt stupid to act this way, as well as not at all being aligned with our vision for Triangl.

We were a totally unknown brand in a reasonably new space, 'online'. It felt really uncomfortable to position ourselves as being a 'good enough' brand to be able to send someone a bikini, and then demand a post in exchange.

We also weren't able to pay anyone to post, because we didn't have the budget, and, again, we didn't want the exchange to be transactional. We paid for one blogger, once, not even via Instagram, and it resulted in mediocre results, which was a relief as we did not want to set up our marketing structure that way.

As I've mentioned earlier, the real drive behind gifting with no expectation of anything in return was because we wanted to build authentic and organic relationships with the girls and women we reached out to. We really wanted them to have a feel-good experience with Triangl, from the moment they received the email, to the moment the bikini arrived, to the moment they tried it on, and – hopefully – loved it. We knew that this flow would be our best chance in getting them to post a photo of the bikini, which is what we wanted, of course! We relied on them sharing our brand, to market it for us via their pages.

We also knew they were more likely to tell their friends of the gift they had received if the whole experience was really personable and positive. And we certainly did not underestimate the power of word of mouth, especially in those early months. Word of mouth is one of the oldest and most tried and tested marketing tools. Creating an experience so wonderful that the customer wanted to tell everyone about it! Every touchpoint had this in mind, and we actually relied on word of mouth as much as we did Instagram initially. Instagram was in a real discovery phase in terms of businesses and brands wanting to use the platform to advertise and market themselves, and didn't have the number of users it does today (nor did we have very many followers!), so we needed a lot of Triangl chat to occur offline too.

The gifting strategy, although it might seem simple, was a comprehensive one. First, I would find like-minded women on Instagram, and what I mean by like-minded was usually that they were bikini girls. Girls who spent time on the beach, who already were taking photos in bikinis for their page, but in a fashion type of way, not in an overtly sexual way. My metrics for this were based off my own intuition, and, I guess, quick judgement of their page. We sometimes went for a girl who wasn't obviously a bikini girl, but who clearly had an interest in fashion, and personal style, but it wasn't as common, more so because we were reliant on receiving photos back from them, taken in a bikini on a beach or by a pool, to then repost on our page and we were much more likely to get that from the bikini girls, not the fashion girls. It was a specific checklist, and one that took a fair amount of time to find the right match. The number of followers didn't really matter all too much; it was more likely we'd get a photo back from a girl with fewer followers anyway after the excitement of being gifted a free bikini. If she had more followers, it was touch and go as to whether she'd be interested and be likely to share a photo at all. We still gifted everyone within these guidelines, but as we were heavily reliant on the images for our own page, getting them from those with smaller followings was an easier task.

Back in 2013, when Instagram was relatively new, things were simpler for users and a bit more challenging for brands. In terms of contacting anyone, we had to comment on the most recent post of theirs in the hopes they'd see it, and ask for their email address, which they then needed to feel comfortable enough to provide. There were no private messages back then, so you had to be really open with your communication, and our comments usually went like this: 'Hi (name), we'd love to get in touch, if you can please let us know your email? Erin x'. But when we spoke to anyone with more of a following, it was: 'Hi (name), we'd love to get in touch, if you can please email erin@triangl.com x'. Or, even more obvious: 'Hi (name), we'd love to send you a bikini, on us! Please let me know your email. Erin x'.

Once I had an email address, or they'd emailed me, the process of sending a bikini was straightforward. They chose the bikini and size, which was a great opportunity to build a relationship over email advising on sizing and colours. Our sizing was XS to XL, so we always needed to explain the conversion to AU or US or EU sizing. We deliberately chose this sizing format for its ability to be understood globally. It also meant we could put only one size on the tag, as opposed to three or four to cover all regions globally, which would have meant a bigger tag, and one that took up significant room on a small bikini top and bottom (each piece needed a tag as we sold sizes separately).

Our response with our gifting strategy was immediately positive; a free bikini with no obligation attached to it was an offer most women were saying yes to. This was only the first step of the process though. Once the bikini arrived, I would often follow up gently with anyone who'd received a Triangl bikini, whether paid for or not. It was more to check in, as at this point I was interested in feedback about the bikini, the packaging, and the delivery time and experience.

Then, we'd wait. As we genuinely didn't expect any Instagram post in return at all, we just had to sit and wait and hope that they would feel inclined to share. Often, they did. And I discovered these posts usually by regularly trawling the pages of the girls we'd gifted bikinis to. I had every reach-out recorded on an Excel spreadsheet, tracking all details so I could be sure not to miss a single potential photo.

When I did find a photo, it was the start of another process in itself. We had a very strict set of guidelines that Craig and I had decided between ourselves. What we'd already noticed on Instagram was that when brands reposted someone wearing their product, they didn't really care how it looked, and just popped it up there, for everyone to see, with the mindset that the social proof was all that mattered.

We did not embody this way of thinking at all, and we saw our Instagram page as being more important than our website. It was where we set the tone of our brand. It was our biggest form of advertising, and our greatest opportunity to highlight what we were about, which was, at the time, fashion-forward designer bikinis for under $100.

If we posted a photo that didn't match this ethos, it just didn't make sense. It looked misaligned, and undesirable for a potential customer, who really needed every interaction with the brand – or at least the ones we could control – to match what we were trying to show. Initially, our guidelines were clear and simple. We wanted the bikini on a body, with white sand and blue water in the picture. We also were happy with blue water, and a clean background. Occasionally, only very occasionally, a clean background was enough, but we really preferred the water element.

We weren't able to do photoshoots often – in fact we did them only rarely – in the early months after launch, so these images we posted had to have the same mood as a photoshoot. This proved to be quite hard, and we didn't receive photos like this very much at all. This resulted in us allowing the addition of a 'flat lay' bikini – the placement of a bikini laid flat. Quite a few girls would take their photos of our bikinis in this way – understandably it was a lot simpler for them to share their photos like this; swimwear on the body takes a level of vulnerability to share!

Flat lays were reminiscent of the Tumblr days; a time before social media where blogs reigned supreme and Tumblr was home to thousands of pages, curated by 'fashion' girls, featuring still images of what inspired them. A blog without words, just images. It was a curated display of a product evoking a feeling of a moment in time. Our bikinis worked really well in a flat lay, as the neoprene especially looked so good laid flat. It was a huge relief to be able to effectively use those images on our page, as the on-model photos were harder to come by in the initial stages of our marketing.

We used to post twice a day, morning and night. Both were set times, the times of most Instagram activity, according to data. This was back in the good old days of the algorithm on Instagram being nothing more than purely chronological, so the more you posted, the more you were seen, full-stop. We didn't want to flood our followers' page with post after post; we saw other brands doing this, but we thought it felt needy, a bit desperate, so we stuck with 8am and 8pm, every single day. I put up every post, regardless of where we were or what we were doing. The only reasons I didn't post were because we were either in China or on a plane.

What we realised after a few months into our Instagram strategy was how we had a few girls who were repeatedly posting our bikinis. And they were doing a great job, so we kept sending bikinis to these girls, knowing it would result in good photos we could reuse. An unspoken agreement if you will. Unbeknown to us, this was the beginning of Triangl's biggest movement on social media, our #trianglgirls.

We had accidentally fallen into this strategy, through the necessity of having to use the same few girls over and over again for new content on our page. But it was a powerful one. Victoria's Secret had their 'angels', but they were the supermodels and there was only a handful of them.

Our Triangl Girls, on the other hand, were just everyday girls. And we found our followers really liked the consistency of seeing the same girls more than once. It felt safe and secure, and built a lot of trust in the brand.

After securing a handful of Triangl Girls in Australia – and by securing I mean sending them bikinis; we never had any kind of formal arrangement in place at all – we started to look overseas. The pool of suitable girls in Australia was small, and even smaller during their winter. The US was just starting their summer, and being such a huge market, we felt like it couldn't hurt to dip our toe in the deep end.

We had enough of a presence online in Australia by now to find girls to send to all over the world, but we knew in the States we had to do something a bit bigger. We'd started receiving international orders only a few months after launch, but it was intermittent, and a far slower burn than it was in Australia, due largely to me not having the familiarity and cut through with the Instagram girls as I did in Australia. We wanted to focus on America, as we knew the bikini business was a big deal there, but we knew it wasn't going to be as easy as it was in Australia. Craig and I had a discussion about who the most well-known person was in the online world at the time. It was already all about the Kardashians. They also jumped on to Instagram in the early days, and were growing rapidly, alongside their reality show.

We didn't want to go after the three big Ks: Kim, Kourtney and Khloé. They were already too old for our main target reach, which was predominantly 15–25-year-olds, and would have certainly required payment. We looked to Kendall and Kylie, who were very young at this point, teenagers still, but building their own personal brands nonetheless. We naturally gravitated towards Kendall; she was the more active of the two sisters and often photographed pool- or beach-side, so we set our sights on her.

Now, we knew we weren't going to be able to get in touch via her Instagram, or even via email – it would have gone unanswered, or with a reply seeking a fee in exchange for post. We had to think outside the square, and lure her in somehow. I was very good at playing Instagram detective by this point, and often deep-dived on a suitable girl's profile to find other girls in her group of friends, or acquaintances. This also usually assisted in the word-of-mouth flow of energy, because if you gifted a bunch of friends separately, they no doubt spoke of it offline as well, and it really helped spread the brand name far and wide.

Adopting this similar process, I went hunting for Kendall's friends. Going through her page, finding her friends, finding their accounts, trying to match up who was friends with who, and who was in the smaller best-mate circle. It wasn't too time-consuming; I did it often. I found about five or six girls, who I was sure were her good friends at the time. Funnily enough, two of them, future celebrities in their own right, Hailey Baldwin (now Bieber) and Bella Hadid, were relative unknowns back then, and only familiar to me as being friends with Kendall. In fact, we had previously gifted Hailey because her sweet girl-next-door American vibe was exactly our usual target girl. Bella was a lot sexier, and I remember wondering if she'd even be interested in our slightly fuller-cut bikini bottoms! However, they were all very happy to be gifted Triangl, and our strike rate of Kendall's circle, in terms of them replying, and also posting in Triangl, was 100 per cent. Now, we just had to sit and wait for Kendall to take the bait. It felt completely far-fetched but completely possible, considering how much I knew the power of girl talk, and that surely they'd all be together by a pool and at some point discuss how they all were sent these bikinis.

As much as Craig and I felt this could actually work, I will never forget the morning I woke up, pulled my laptop onto my lap, checking my emails as I always did, and found an email from a gmail account with the name kennykillerrrr or something similar (no, I didn't keep the email!), and I just knew straight away, without even reading it, that it was Kendall Jenner, and our fanciful plan to woo her had worked.

It said something along the lines of 'Hi! My friends were all sent these really cute bikinis. I'd love to get some too!'

BOOM. Hook, line and sinker. This was no doubt one of the most pivotal moments for Triangl.

Craig and I knew this was big. And we had a huge opportunity. We subsequently sent her the entire collection (we had to make up for being slightly mean and leaving her out in front of her friends!), and, sure enough, she tweeted (her Twitter following was five million – at the time bigger than her Instagram following) and shared our Instagram handle: @triangl.

And that was really it for us. I believe we would have continued our pace of getting into the market in the US, as we were an Australian swimwear brand, which, due to our well-known summer loving, beachy culture, meant we already had some kind of authority over how to produce a good bikini, and had a style of bikini commercial enough to suit the mainstream bikini girl. But Kendall's support accelerated our growth rapidly. It really was the start of a wild three-year period of growth.

The social proof of Kendall wearing the bikinis (which she quite often did, giving us more exposure every time), created a flow-on effect. Everything Kendall wore and did resulted in numerous publications writing it up, and, sure enough, this small brand 'Triangl', which she was seen wearing on occasion, got written up too. Soon afterwards our brand was worn by Kylie, Kim, Kourtney and even Kris. The Kardashian effect was, indeed, very real. We were being written up daily by all the social commentary sites, as well as constantly reposted by fan pages, and their apparent authority in popular culture paved the way for every other celebrity to accept and embrace Triangl as the go-to bikini brand. This kind of presence, combined with our continued influencer strategy of gifting regular girls and with the product being desirable, was the magic combination for us.

Being propelled into the American market meant we had to scramble to set up a new website, in the Northern Hemisphere summer of 2014. We wanted to host a site in US dollars and make it easy for the region to shop in a way that felt safe and local. We set up two additional websites: one for North America and one 'International', which was primarily for Europe and the UK but was hosted in US dollars. This wasn't something we put much time into, admittedly, as the International site would have needed to be split into GBP, EUR, USD and all other currencies to capture the rest of the world, and we quite simply were far too under resourced to be able to split the site up to serve our customers outside of the US and Australia. We were certainly very focused on the US, and while we did experience notable growth and online success in the UK and Europe at the same time as the US growth, we never reached our full potential or sustained those regions, due to our focus being so directed towards the US.

The decision to relocate to Sydney for the summer of 2013–14 was with the intention of staying in Bondi to shoot as much as possible for our social media and website. The business was expanding rapidly by this point, and while we wanted to spend the summer in Australia, it became clear rather quickly that it wasn't going to be a leisurely summer, and that we'd be working pretty solidly.

We had a bunch of new styles we needed to photograph, as well as wanting to launch an underwear range – a category we'd both been invested in and one that very easily came to fruition, using our new factory in China, which specialised in lingerie and underwear.

Our new underwear was not dissimilar to the famous black-binding look Triangl was becoming well known for. We used a beautifully soft mesh and released two styles: a triangle bralette and a balconette.

Our rented apartment in Sydney was right across the road from Bondi Beach, the perfect place to shoot, and we did – almost every single day.

We contacted models in Sydney, most of whom were already Triangl Girls (#trianglgirls) anyway, but some we scouted on the streets or on the beaches and arranged to shoot them for a few hours for both the swimwear and new underwear collection, starting at 6.30am on the beach. The lighting at this time of day was soft, and the beach was never too busy.

The models would come to the apartment ready to go, no need for hair and makeup (natural was always better and more realistic anyway for swimwear) and we would walk down to the beach – Craig with his camera and me with the bikinis and towels and a lighting reflector. Craig and I did every shoot ourselves, until almost the end of 2014, when we were already making millions. When I say we kept the business lean, this is what I mean. We did almost everything ourselves, for as long as possible.

The models would change into the different bikinis on the beach and I'd surround them with towels during the changes to protect their modesty. Then we'd head up to the apartment and photograph them in the underwear range, in the back room against a white wall. We'd be done by 9am usually, and be able to enjoy a few hours on the beach, work for a few hours, beach and repeat. We did this for weeks, and built quite the catalogue of images.

We launched the underwear in early 2014, following the same gifting strategy, and using our own fairly strong swimwear following on Instagram. It was an immediate success.

The brand identity for the underwear was a bit more 'cool girl', and we were able to differentiate it enough from the swimwear girl so they didn't dilute each other, while still maintaining enough similarities to keep it all under one brand name.

One thing that worked really well with the underwear was the desire for friends to get matching sets. Every time we posted on our Instagram, girls would comment under the posts to talk about their plans over what to buy. They would discuss at length which bikini they would get, but they had to ensure there were minimal clashes, so every girl needed to get a different one. But underwear was different, and it was very acceptable to match with your friends, and that seemed to be quite the drawcard.

In spite of all of this, with swimwear growing at the rate it was in 2014, which I can't even put a figure on, but it felt like it was on a sharp incline every day, we chose to close the underwear brand down. Quite simply, we did not have the resources to be able to do it all ourselves, and aside from a merchandiser in China, and a merchandiser based in Hong Kong, it was still all Craig and me doing everything, and there was no way to manage the operations of the underwear without it having some kind of detrimental impact on the swimwear, which was absolutely not an option at all as far as we were concerned.

It felt wrong to remove a successful offshoot of the business, but it wasn't worth the risk of impacting Triangl negatively. We needed to be completely and wholly focused on Triangl, and as it really was just two of us, it meant there was no time or room for basically anything else.

We couldn't even bring anyone in to run the underwear line, as that would have involved training someone up and we didn't even have the time to spare to do that.

It wasn't a decision we ever regretted, due to the massive success of Triangl Swimwear, but it was one I sometimes wondered about, and what may have been if we could have continued building up Triangl Underwear.

~

While we had been shooting different shapes and releasing new styles from Sydney in early 2014, they were only different tops. The bottom shape was the same. A hipster bottom, a classic bikini shape. The Australian market was satisfied with this shape and we never had any complaints. However, it was in these early months I was noticing more comments from our American customers, imploring us to make a cheeky bottom. We were dead against it initially, as it didn't feel very on brand for aligning with our Triangl aesthetic.

I read the comments on our Instagram religiously, every single comment on every post, and I answered every single question, whether negative or positive. It was a very important part of our strategy, to be active on our Instagram as much as I possibly could. I would even read comments on other pages where women posted our swimwear, and also replied there if a question was asked or comment was made. I was focused on being the most active brand on Instagram, not only because it resulted in sales ultimately, but because it was where we learned so much about what our customers thought of us.

And one request that kept coming up was the 'cheeky bottom'. The American customers were finding our bottoms really full, and a bit daggy. They were relentless in commenting 'make a cheeky bum'. I was so across all the commentary that I knew this was something worth investigating, so we sampled and fitted a more 'cheeky' bum – one we felt comfortable doing. I was never personally a cheeky kind of girl; however, I recall vividly that moment when I first tried them, and they were so flattering. Assuming a cheeky bum would make your bum look bigger as it was less fabric, I was so surprised to find it made my bum look smaller, perkier and somehow just better. We immediately put a production order through and added 'cheeky bum' as an option to our bikini styles. It immediately sold, and sales of normal vs cheeky were 50/50 and eventually in favour of the cheeky.

This was something we would have missed if I hadn't been so active on social media and involved with my customers. As a founder, your vison needs to be strong, and you need to hold the objective of finding and maintaining your niche. But it's a fine line between holding strong on who you want to be versus letting go of the chokehold and allowing for customers to help shape and curate the offering, if it's something that could really allow you to grow.

The addition of the cheeky bottom was a perfect example of this for us. Expanding our offering, and letting go of the reins just a little, allowed our customer base to grow in the US even more strongly. It was a nod to that market, and cemented our position in the US as a must-have bikini brand.

Chapter Seven

Scaling Up

We returned to Hong Kong in February 2014. We'd found consistency in our social-media strategy, and our manufacturing model, which was built around releasing new arrivals every few weeks, was humming along. It allowed for a little bit more of a balance, in terms of our workload.

I was able to hire a customer-care manager for North America, Jodie. I spent over a month training her over video calls, ensuring she understood exactly how I spoke, how I handled comments, how I managed every part of the customer journey. Jodie was in Canada, and we found her on ODesk (now known as Upwork). Working from home, Jodie took on the role with such ownership, and was the perfect person to speak for me. She was such a lovely woman, and I thoroughly enjoyed working alongside her. What we were doing felt much more than customer care; we'd given Jodie authority to be a leader, to have ownership and pride over what she was doing. By this stage, we had 24/7 Live Chat, emails that were replied to within one hour at all times of the day and a fully manned Instagram, where every comment was replied to and followed up on.

It was too much for Jodie and me alone, and so we hired a number of women from the Philippines via ODesk. At first, I was a little unsure this was the right way to go about it, in terms of best practices and ethics involved. However, the women we met online, and got to know, and then went and visited later on that year in Manila, were the most special group of women I'd ever encountered. Working from home, raising families, these women became my closest confidantes, and I became theirs. Teaching them how to speak the Triangl way and educating them on the importance of the customer and the experience allowed for so many of these women to upskill, to find the confidence to get more out of their lives and to move on, when they felt ready to. The gratitude these women had towards being able to work, combined with a level of ambition I was not used to in Australia, made for a very comfortable transition for me out of having to handle most of the customer care, as by then it just wasn't manageable anymore.

We were getting thousands of comments on some posts, hundreds of emails a day, and Live Chat queues usually hovered between thirty to fifty women, for twenty hours a day. While it became necessary for me to let go, and even with the confidence in my Filipina team of women, letting go of this connection with my customers had a monumentally detrimental impact on me, one which I couldn't determine until years later.

Letting go of my customer relationships was swiftly replaced with all the other admin that was growing in size every day.

Craig and I spent most of 2014 shooting the images ourselves for our website and social media, almost always in Bali, being only five hours by air from Hong Kong. The logistics involved in photoshoots alone were enough to be a full-time job, and one I continued organising through the years. It was an overwhelmingly stressful job. We'd moved from scouting girls on the street or Instagram to primarily booking models through an agency, which made for a more professional process, but also meant managing agents, talent, venues, permits, samples, edits, payments – it never ended, as we were shooting every few weeks and it kept me up at night far too many times to count.

It was a difficult role in terms of the energy it took for business negotiations, as agents were always quoting rates we couldn't afford, and everything else was about budgets and money. I had to get way out of my comfort zone in negotiating, which felt unnatural and uncomfortable to me. I missed my safe place of supporting customers in feeling good about a bikini, and while I oversaw all the customer-care employees and was still approving all gifting myself, my direct connection with my customers was gone, and it felt like the biggest hole in my heart.

While this sense of emotional loss was very slowly unfolding, without my being aware really at all of it happening (the perks and pitfalls of being so busy every day), Craig and I were able to achieve more balance in our personal lives as we outsourced more of our business commitments.

We arrived back to our apartment at Four Seasons in early 2014, and not long after this, we bought a very small boat to enjoy the beaches in Hong Kong more often.

When we had first moved to Hong Kong, I was struck by how many beaches there were, which were on the Hong Kong Island, but the other side of the city. There were the densest green forests, leading on to actual real beaches with sand. Sure, the water was often as flat as a lake, and as warm as a bath, and often the pollution haze was so bad you couldn't really see the sun, but there were still beaches, and visiting them was a popular weekend activity within the expat community.

We liked this time so much that only a few months after the initial boat purchase, we bought a bigger boat. A 65-metre-long, 3-bedroom boat. It was the most luxurious purchase we'd ever made, and it felt so special. We hired a captain, and would head out almost every weekend to spend a few days switching off, something neither Craig nor I had been able to do for more than an hour or two for the past two years.

As much as I truly enjoyed these trips, something really shifted in these months for me. I began to feel like Triangl was outgrowing me. I didn't know where I was going to fit in to the business as it continued to grow rapidly. It was an internal imposter syndrome experience, and one which most likely could have been squashed fairly quickly if I'd had the mental-health tools to process it myself, or if I'd been able to verbalise it to someone else. But I didn't tell anyone. I felt so ashamed that I wasn't fully loving what I was doing anymore during this incredible period of success. I really just felt so lonely.

We'd been away from friends and family for two years by this stage, and I barely spoke to anyone anymore. I'd been so unbelievably frantic for all of 2013 that I'd killed off most of my friendships from back home. And my family, I felt, were just so sick of hearing about our success every day. It felt like we reached a new milestone every week in 2014.

One million followers on Instagram. One million dollars in the bank. While it should have been an exuberant time, knowing we'd created all this for ourselves, I was finding it really hard to feel more than a surface-level acknowledgement of what was happening. I missed connection. I missed my life in Australia. I missed my customers.

Of course, it wasn't constant misery for me, and there were many times of happiness, excitement, fulfilment and joy, but they were forever being met with feelings of discontentment, insecurity, loneliness and shame over feeling anything negative at all.

I was suffering greatly in my mind, and, without any knowledge of how to share it, I hid it.

I coped in two ways. The first was to drink at every opportunity I could. I was never a big drinker, and I still wasn't at all. I never drank outside of accepted times or got blackout drunk. I was just using alcohol as a tool to try and ignite happiness. Ignite a feeling of gratitude for what was happening around me – the success we were having. I was obsessed with the idea of stopping, relaxing and enjoying myself, for a moment. It naturally extended to alcohol as I'd always had a good relationship with drinking before Triangl times, back home in Melbourne. It had always been fun, joyful and a moment of connection with friends. A mood-booster for me before I'd lived in Hong Kong.

I became fixated on the thought of having a drink almost all day long, every day. I obsessed over the idea of it. In Hong Kong, people drink a lot. It was around me wherever I went, and I would walk past people drinking all the time and long to be one of them or be with them. To be able to sit there and relax. I wanted to feel good. I wanted to feel relaxed. This was the only way I ever felt I could. This attempted act of escapism stayed with me for years and years.

The other coping mechanism I had relied on for so long, and which was arguably more damaging, was my disordered eating. As I'd come into starting Triangl as a bulimic on the verge of somewhat recovering, stepping back into these obsessive thought patterns and behaviours felt easy. During a time of feeling totally out of control with all my other thoughts, my eating was the one thing I could be in control of. I began purging again, but mainly I just didn't eat. I used food as a weapon, and I controlled my calorie intake to be very low every day. I rarely stepped outside of this framework I'd set up, and I punished myself immensely if I did. I reserved purging for times when I felt really stressed, as the act itself was so exhausting that it took away so many of my chaotic thoughts and left me feeling numb, which was relaxing to me, at the time. I was also abusing laxatives excessively, taking them after almost every meal, resulting in horrific bloating and stomach pain. I was truly addicted to laxatives, and this was the scariest part of this time with my disorder – I knew they were causing a lot of damage. While I'd been able to get on top of my bulimia once before, I'd never had something so physical take a hold on me.

I used to google at night and read horror stories about young women who had kidney failure after stopping laxatives, or not been able to ever use their bowels again. So I was both terrified to keep going and terrified to stop. It was an all-consuming mental battle. And one I had to daily get somewhat on top of to be able to continue pushing Triangl to more and more success.

My eating disorder was so much more a mental battle than physical. I used to look in the mirror during periods of relaxing my boundaries and eating more – usually when we had friends stay with us, or went on a trip to shoot – and I liked my body more when it had more fuel in it. I felt better on a physical and logical level, but the mental toxicity of needing 'control' would always win. As soon as I felt a moment of insecurity, frustration, doubt or anger at myself or anyone else, the coping mechanism of restricting or purging food pushed itself to the forefront of my mind.

It was a heartbreaking feeling, to know I felt better being and looking healthy but that my mind didn't know how to switch into feeling that way permanently. I'd developed this internal programming and pattern to revert to punishment mode as soon as I was triggered in any way that was at all negative.

Of course, this was all internalised, and I never directly voiced my concerns to anyone. I had to work so hard in my mind to maintain a relatively positive and happy disposition, and to keep working at the rate that we were. However, I often would fly into periods of total shutdown, complete breakdown. I'd cry and fret so often at what appeared on the surface as almost nothing, but of course to me it always felt like the final straw. It could be such a small thing that would send my world into total disarray.

Naturally, this was putting enormous pressure on Craig and my working relationship, not to mention on our personal relationship. He could hardly say a word, or even make a facial expression, without me reacting strongly over it. Not wanting to cause any huge conflict, I never properly addressed my issues for fear over what it could mean for our relationship, and also for Triangl. So I kept it all in.

~

We were releasing many new shapes in 2014, and we had a lot of freedom over what we put into the market. By then, neoprene was our 'hook' – what people were discovering our brand for – so we were able to play with new ideas.

We had been working on a balconette-style bikini top for a while as it was a shape we used for our underwear range, and it was very popular with both smaller and bigger busts, being a mould cup that shaped and supported breasts really well. As we were already known for our black binding that ran along the borders of our bikini tops and bottoms, we put this on the top. It was a striking look, and very bold. We called it 'Milly', and released it in the middle of the year. It was an immediate hit, playing straight into the shaping benefits of the neoprene.

From this point, our biggest challenge became keeping up with the volume of the sales coming through and ensuring our production model was running efficiently.

We had finally committed to an office and had hired a few staff members, largely to support the supply chain and also to manage accounts from a financial perspective. Up until then, it had just been Craig and me, our merchandiser and an old business acquaintance of Craig who assisted with logistics and the supply chain. This extremely lean setup was why Triangl was so heavily profitable from almost day one. But while it was a fantastic setup financially, it was too much in terms of workload, and whenever we held a meeting with any external provider, they were gobsmacked and in almost disbelief over the lack of staff and infrastructure at Triangl. We were making millions of dollars in revenue, with a team of two, and a few other contractors handling the necessary accounting and supply-chain management.

As I've mentioned earlier, Craig had based the business off *The Lean Startup*. For the record, my only understanding of this book is via Craig's recounting of it to me, as I never read it myself. But for me, the title is self-explanatory. Lean startup: doing anything and everything yourself, for as long as you can. We had a rare experience in which our business grew so fast that staying lean meant we each had to take on several roles ourselves in the business. This was initially a conscious decision, which continued because our growth happened fast that we didn't have any time to think about recruiting other people. Without any other staff or team to lean on, and with very slim pickings in Hong Kong to bring in any kind of administrative help quickly (we needed to find expats with experience in the Western world, and they were all working in finance and not interested in us), the responsibility for every business decision was on us. We spread ourselves too thinly, but it was also hard to let go of, considering having very little overheads for staff or external agencies (marketing/PR/supply-chain agents) meant our profit margins were through the roof. That is, we were making, and keeping, a lot of money.

Our first office was in the commercial area of Wan Chai, a whole floor of an office building, which Craig had gutted and was fitting out from scratch. A little side project of his, he sourced beautiful furniture and created an exquisite space for our team to work from.

We had to focus largely on automating processes as quickly as possible at this point (we had a significant lack of them, due to eighteen months of hectic, desperate scaling). This was a tedious undertaking, and the first time Triangl really felt like work to me. Sitting all day long in meeting after meeting, detailing every single process we had in place step by step, from customer care, to logistics, to accounts, to operations as a whole.

It was also the same time that I found out I was pregnant. I'd been off the pill since not long after I met Craig back in Melbourne. Being ten years older than me, he was keen to start a family soon and I'd had a gut feeling it may take a while for me to fall pregnant, due to my years of disordered eating and the effect I felt it was having on my body.

I had already seen a specialist obstetrician in Hong Kong a few months prior to becoming pregnant. Because it had been almost three years since I'd come off the pill, and we were using no other contraception, the question had been raised of something perhaps being not quite right.

The obstetrician ran some tests, asked some questions, asked me to monitor my cycle closely and told me to come back in three months if I hadn't fallen pregnant.

The thing was, I wasn't often getting my period back then, most likely due to my bulimia, anorexia and laxative abuse. I told my OB this, in full confidence, and his reply was that I may still be ovulating, so to take note of my cycle over the next few months and then return if nothing happened.

I remember feeling so relieved voicing to someone that I was not well, and his reaction was so practical that it felt quite empowering. I mean, it was obvious to me that I was having trouble becoming pregnant because I was extremely unhealthy, both physically and mentally, and I knew I had to try and overcome that, albeit temporarily.

I told myself I'd relax with my obsessive behaviour around food, and all my negative thoughts, and that I'd be allowed to pick them up again and return to my normal punish–restrict mentality after I had a baby. I only felt like I relaxed a small amount, in terms of letting go, but it was apparently enough for my body to allow a pregnancy in. The exact day I found out I was having a baby was the day I then stopped taking laxatives and stopped purging. It was the easiest decision because it was made for me. It wasn't about me anymore, and there was not a chance I was going to do anything more selfish than I already was, and risk that little life of my child.

In what felt like an accurate representation of the tumultuous relationship between Craig and I we had a huge argument the day I found out I was pregnant. I was in bed, absolutely exhausted, and this was met with dismay by Craig, which always led to the same argument, a mismatch of values. Him wanting to work around the clock on Triangl, in spite of everything else life had to offer, and me wanting a fucking break for a day. He stormed out after a screaming match, and I lay there crying, in total despair, but also realizing suddenly how much bigger my breasts were, and how sore they were.

I trudged off to do a pregnancy test, wondering if perhaps my recent exhaustion was down to this, and indeed – it was. I sent Craig a perhaps spiteful text message with a photo of the positive test, and as always the same, we moved forward without properly addressing our ever-increasing differences.

Wanting to start this new chapter of my life fresh, and reeling from a bout of arguments Craig and I were having, me navigating pretty hectic pregnancy nausea and exhaustion, and Craig not understanding how this meant I needed to pull back from work, I sought out something big to do, and travelled solo to India to spend a week at a meditation retreat. This was the first kind of real self-development work I'd ever done. And in true Erin style, I had jumped straight into the deep end. I was five weeks pregnant at the time, and spent the week immersed in the retreat. However, I did hold back to an extent, as I knew I had to because I just wasn't ready to deal with acknowledging the lack of fulfilment I felt in my life. I felt that admitting my struggles would mean the end for Craig and me, which I felt would kill Triangl in an instant. And I knew I couldn't be responsible for that. I felt sick at the thought of disrupting our lives at that point, at any point really, but especially not while Triangl was on the trajectory it was.

My nervous system had calmed down a lot, though, during the retreat, and I returned home in a good mental place. I felt refreshed to an extent, and even hopeful that it had been enough to shut those negative feelings down forever.

~

I was blessed with a really good pregnancy. I had fairly standard nausea for the first few months, but was able to work from home, on the couch, and I remember that time fondly.

I felt like I had no pressure on me anymore; all the pressure I'd applied to myself had dissipated. And it was so nice to just relax and lean into it.

I worked really hard on operations for the few months following my time in India.

Letting go of the customer-care part of the business opened up so much space for me to do anything else I wanted, and I immersed myself in the processes, fine-tuning everything I could. The work I was doing was quite repetitive but I found it fairly easy. I differentiated my work time or 'on' time from my leisure or 'off' time, and I liked having that separation. I'd missed the simplicity of a normal work–life routine, and I had it back during these months. It felt like I worked for Triangl at times, as opposed to it being my business, but I found that soothing.

In November 2014, we decided it was time to arrange our first proper professional photoshoot. One that involved a world-class photographer, world-class model and world-class editing. We felt the brand deserved something really incredible, special, different – and we felt it would really make an impact on our customers to see something so polished. We had a new style to release as well, the 'Poppy' bikini.

Poppy was the same shape as the Milly, but it was colour blocked and had different coloured panels on both the bikini top and bottom. Somehow, it was bolder than the Milly. We had chosen three colours for each bikini. It was eye-catching but we'd gone with a pastel palette so it somehow looked really soft and feminine at the same time.

We locked in our photographer, Darren McDonald, an Australian photographer who we'd seen doing great things, and the model Georgia

Fowler, who was early on in her career at the time, but it was a career that was about to go big.

We shot off the coast of Lombok, in the Gili Islands. I didn't go to this particular shoot but stayed in Hong Kong to keep working on systems and processes. I was happy to stay home and leave Craig to oversee the shoot.

Darren had a way of evoking such beauty in his images and the result was so polished, so refined, so luxurious, and the bikinis looked incredible.

We released the Poppy bikini, and it went – and there is no better word to describe it – nuts! The photoshoot of that bikini sent sales to the moon. It was the biggest turning point for Triangl. We had been catapulted into being one of the most desirable brands in the world, especially on Instagram, and everyone wanted a piece of Triangl, and a piece of Craig and me.

Chapter Eight

My Oscar

We flew back to Australia for Christmas 2014. This trip was short and it felt almost uncomfortable to be back there. We were Australians by birth, yet I felt far removed from my previous life in Australia now. It wasn't for lack of trying, and we visited with my family, as well as Craig's dad and mum. Everyone was excited for us in regard to both our business and our future baby, but we felt disconnected. Our lives were so different to anyone else's; we were living a totally unique life, utterly committed to Triangl and this new life it was giving us. Aside from the baby's pending arrival, we weren't living a life anyone could understand. Engaged but with absolutely no plans to get married (how would we ever find time to fit it in?), and with nothing else to talk of except our meteoric rise to wealth and success. It wasn't even really a conscious thing, and it wasn't me feeling superior, but I just didn't feel like it was 'home' anymore. We had nothing to relate to in Melbourne, and no one really wanted to hear our success story over and over and over again. Whether that was actually true, or perhaps it was more because I felt like I had to dull my light so others wouldn't feel uncomfortable, it wasn't a very nice feeling and we only stayed for a week or so.

This sense of separation from my hometown, where my identity had been built, was incredibly tough. I was already suffering from my loss of passion, purpose and sense of self – and to have it magnified in a place I had known as 'home' was really unsettling, and naturally perpetuated my sadness.

Returning to Hong Kong didn't feel like going home either, and while we sought comfort in the hustle and bustle of the city, and in our work, the isolation from everyone and everything seemed greater than ever.

I had absolutely no one to talk to, which, of course, wasn't true, but to me it felt like it was. I was so afraid to share with anyone how I really felt, how I was lonely, how I felt misplaced, how I was still sick – it would have felt like admitting the truth of how useless I was. It was easier to pretend I was living this dream life and not deal with anything piling up inside my mind.

And, of course, we had this incredibly successful business to keep me busy enough or pretend to be focused on.

The reality was that by this point the business was running itself in the sense of the switch had been flipped, where we went from being a business that was all about reaching outwards to a business that everyone was reaching into.

Everyone on social media wanted to be a Triangl Girl, and every publication in Australia, the UK and the US was turning their focus on to this swimwear brand that had seemingly exploded into the world out of nowhere. We were still actively reaching out to social-media influencers, as I refused to abandon this part of the business, even though it was probably not necessary anymore due to all the incoming attention. I felt the flow of energy had to stay the same, though. I was worried that if we stopped gifting the 'micro influencers' (I put this in quote marks because we never used that term but it refers to when you gift anyone with a small following), the shift would be detrimental, and that people would come after us, saying we were getting too big for our boots.

It was something I was fiercely protective of, ensuring we kept our strategies just as they had always been. I felt it was largely why Triangl had this good feeling about it, because we were a brand for everyone, and even when being worn by the biggest celebrities in the world, we were gifting our regular girls all over the world.

It did feel a little odd, to be cross-checking the Excel spreadsheet daily of influencer reach-outs, while fielding emails from a stylist requesting a bikini for Beyoncé, and seeing yet another Victoria's Secret angel wearing Triangl. But it was important to me, even though it was a role that took a lot of time, and adding that to the now full-time management of inbound queries via social media – a role which I held myself solely accountable for, and refused to let go of – my workload was out of control and also predominantly admin, which was fast becoming tedious and lonely, with the thrill of the chase of the influencer long gone. Now, I was left with a robotic process where I sent bikinis to girls basically pleading for them.

I also felt like I'd gotten nowhere in implementing new processes and automated systems within the business. It was still just Craig and I when it came to fundamental operations of the business. We had a lot of support under us but no one to be able to sit with us, at the table, initiating strategies or structures. I found all attempts at putting a new workflow into practice impossible. Craig and I had to agree on all systems to move forward, which was rare, and while it was our biggest superpower in the first years to always have opposing views over a certain bikini design, or the flow of a page of the website, because it drove Triangl to be the best it could be, it was now working against us in terms of putting any infrastructure in place.

I became loath to mention anything I wanted to do, as it always resulted in an argument and never moved forward after that. An example of this was automating our returns system. Something that kept me awake at night was knowing that customers had to take their bikini to the post office and return it themselves, a totally manual process that I knew was not in line with my dedication to the customer journey being at the forefront of all we focused on.

I knew automated returns were possible, which was where the customer could return an unwanted bikini by simply clicking on a link on our website to generate a shipping document and label, to be then passed over a desk at the post office, as opposed to seeking and writing and paying for the return in the post office, and I'd done plenty of research on who was doing them well. I'd arrange meetings, and talk to the third-party providers of these platforms, alongside Craig, who would ask a bunch of questions, usually regarding costs (and his unwillingness to pay them), which totally derailed my attempts to move forward. This left everything unresolved, as I had not factored in another bunch of meetings, or back-and-forths, and needed to continue managing my excessively large workload.

We were missing that person to assist with the implementation of these kinds of logistical, structural facets of the business, and so it felt these ideas went round in circles and were never put into practice – that they remained as an idea for another day. Of course, this made me feel utterly useless, and I was increasingly turning my resentment and frustration on Craig, who was also just trying his very best to stay on top of everything.

Our website was hosted on Shopify, which was the most fantastic platform for us. We had found a web developer in the UK who was the most diligent, hardworking and kind man – and kept everything running smoothly and cohesively. We were also using PayPal as our only payment merchant, which was another platform we relied heavily on, and they were very good to us.

These two established platforms helped keep us so lean and nimble at the start, and allowed us to grow the business without managing a website or handling payments directly, which would have been an involved set of ongoing responsibilities.

The issue we were finding as we became a global business was that our superpower in our first year or two, of keeping everything between Craig and me where possible, was working against us. We had no one to sit alongside us, actively participating in the business to allow the growth to expand and evolve.

Our developer saw these issues, and would send us plug-in apps he had seen on Shopify, which were there to streamline the process somewhat and take the leg work out of planning, but due to a total lack of having anyone to work on operations or logistics, they were never implemented.

We were selling around 1000 pairs of swimwear a day at this stage, so while it was incredibly frustrating to never feel we were able to level up our processes, the sales were enough to push those issues to the background.

We were travelling a lot as well, for both work and play – our budget had dramatically increased for photoshoots, and we were back in Bali as well as in Los Angeles and Palm Springs in those first few months of 2015. These trips always put a real stop to my workflow, and I found it hard to stay consistent with anything while we were away, with the time-zone changes and changes in routine.

I was well into my pregnancy and was having a very easy experience and time with it. However, these trips away were very detrimental in terms of my disordered eating and mental health because my issues around control, or lack thereof, were more apparent when I was away from home. I became fixated on controlling and restricting my food again, and this took up a lot of space in my mind.

I really didn't want to put on a ton of weight in this pregnancy, and this type of thinking started another wave of my eating issues. The anxiety over every impending meal, the management of what I'd eaten versus how much I'd walked that day, and the very real problem of what this may be doing to my unborn child were all so much to manage, and it left only the bare minimum of energy in terms of my efforts towards Triangl. Fortunately, this was enough at the time, anyway, as the brand was cruising. I felt like my absolutely huge efforts in setting up the success of the business gave me grace to take my foot off the pedal for a little while. Perhaps this was true, but it definitely should not have happened without anyone else to pick up the slack on behalf of me.

I knew this in the back of my mind, but, like I knew to do so well, those thoughts stayed buried deep down.

~

We had moved apartments in Hong Kong, again, in early 2015 to a beautiful building right in the heart of the Central business district, called Pacific Place. Admittedly it was not dissimilar to the Four Seasons Place, being yet another lovely building, where our apartment was serviced and cleaned every day, and with yet another shopping mall directly below, but the rooms were bigger, which we thought suited our soon to be family of three better, and also I liked the shopping in this mall more than in the other one.

Due to my severe lack of naturally happy feelings and moments, I sought the hit of dopamine through shopping. I'd never had money like this before and was completely obsessed with spending it to make me feel better. The shops were also the only place I had real connection with anyone. I'd stopped going into our office by this point, blaming it on the exhaustion of my pregnancy but, really, I was finding it too disheartening to experience the same merry-go-round of getting nothing done because of the way Craig and I worked together despite the fact I had a million ideas of what we needed to do.

Cruising the shops was how I felt connection, and how I felt marginally happy again.

I'd always been obsessed with personal style and fashion, and shopping – whether it be vintage, high street or luxury – was something that really once brought me joy. However, I'd taken this joyful time and turned it into something dangerous and toxic, but didn't know how to stop. I didn't know how to get it back to being a true passion of mine, so I just ignored those shameful feelings of excessive purchasing and spending, and kept doing it. It's something I now still have to check in with myself the most about, over any other toxic behaviour, and I feel I'll always need to, as my shopping behaviour has manifested as treading the finest line between healthy, joyful moments and obsessive, excessive, toxic times.

Craig was travelling back and forth between Bali and Hong Kong quite a bit during this time because we'd acquired some land to build a home on – a long-time dream of his, and one I went along with but most certainly resented him for. I resented him for having dreams that felt like they were being fulfilled, whereas I didn't know what any of mine were.

It was a huge relief for me whenever he left Hong Kong, which I, at the time, thought was because of my issues with him, but on reflection have realised was because of my issues with myself, and that I wanted to fully indulge in my toxic behaviours without feeling like I had to hide them from him.

I was just under six weeks out from my due date when Craig left for Bali for another trip. The night before he left, I was complaining of cramps, and how they felt like they were coming and going. But I was so intent on him leaving the next day that I brushed them off as nothing serious, and he left that next morning.

I was still in quite a bit of pain, but I'd always saved my shopping for when Craig was away, and I wasn't going to let these cramps stop me. I headed downstairs and into YSL to buy a pair of ankle boots I'd been thinking about getting. I didn't even try them on; I just bought them. I had this sudden overpowering urge to get back to the apartment. I felt like something really wasn't right, and shopping was not going to drown the noise out this time.

I returned to the safety of my quiet apartment and sat down, willing the cramps to subside. After some time, I decided to try my boots on, and sat at the dining-room table to do so. Leaning down to open the shoe box, putting some pressure on my very pregnant belly, I heard a loud *pop!*, and liquid started pouring out from between my legs.

Being five-and-a-half weeks from my due date, it didn't cross my mind that perhaps I may be in labour, and all my fears of the damage I was doing to this baby in previous months rushed to the surface. I called my obstetrician's office, and was directed to a voicemail where I screamed down the line, 'It's Erin Deering and something is very wrong. I think my baby is dying!' I then proceeded to call my older sister, Bree, who, thank god, picked up the phone. I was less hysterical at this point, and, with a towel between my legs that I'd run and taken from the bathroom, I told her what had happened, to which she replied very calmly, 'Erin, your water has broken – you're in labour.' The relief of this was *huge*, and I started laughing, which shifted the pure fear that had been coursing through my body prior to this realisation.

I had bought hardly a single baby item at this point, let alone packed a hospital bag. I ran around our apartment, giggling out of sheer shock, stuffing undies, shorts, skincare and bras into a large tote bag.

I got off the phone and stepped into action mode. I tried to call Craig, which was a pointless move as he was on his plane to Bali by then. I then called the concierge at the front desk to request a taxi to take me to the hospital. Explaining with some urgency why I needed to get there fast, the concierge swiftly took care of the taxi and within two minutes was at my front door with a wheelchair and the girl from the front desk of our building, Amy, to take me down to the waiting taxi. Still with a towel between my legs, I was wheeled into a taxi, where both the concierge and Amy insisted that she go with me to the hospital to ensure I got there safely and without incident. I will never forget the kindness they showed me when I was all alone, facing the realisation I was going to have my first baby without my partner or any other friend or family member there, and it brings more than a tear to my eye to remember how cared for I felt.

I was having the baby at Matilda International Hospital, which was at the Peak in Hong Kong, which, as the name suggests, is at the top of the mountain overlooking the whole of Hong Kong Island and the South China Sea. The trip could take anywhere from fifteen to fifty minutes, depending on the time of the day, and fortunately, being the middle of the day, we were on the lesser side, which was extremely fortunate as my contractions, which had been practically non-existent when my water broke (due to being in shock), suddenly went to a 10/10 level of pain. I was unable to talk, open my eyes or process anything other than managing the pain.

Breathing through it as best I could, we arrived at the top of the Peak and Amy got the staff to come out and wheel me straight through to a room, and then stayed with me to help fill out the paperwork as I had no one else there to do it for me. She left shortly after this, and I thanked her for being there for me, while quietly wishing she could stay and hold my hand.

I remember getting stripped out of my clothes and put into a gown, and I lay on the bed.

I finally called my mum, back in Melbourne, who had spoken to my sister, so knew what was going on.

I'd planned a fully natural birth, and was 100 per cent set on it being that way, but I had not done any preparation for how to manage the pain. The contractions were coming fast, and they were the most painful thing I'd ever felt or could imagine feeling. The pain radiated through my whole body in a way I didn't even think possible, and somehow encapsulated the pain my mind had been in for years by bringing it into the physical. It was torture. I was grabbing onto the side of the bed, without any time to process what was happening as the contractions were already only ninety seconds apart. My poor mum, who had stayed on the phone with me, had to endure my tortured cries and screams without being able to be there for me, and since becoming a mother, I now truly know the mental agony she would have been in during this whole experience.

My obstetrician turned up and, having been briefed on what was happening, made things very clear to me immediately. 'Erin, I know the plan was no epidural, but you're going to have this baby on your own, and this is not the time to be a hero.'

I immediately felt so grateful to have been told what to do in this moment, and very quickly the anaesthetist was in the room. He cruised in, a local doctor in a brown leather jacket, coming from a lunch and acting very cavalier. These details I remember clearly because he was the beacon of light, the man who was going to give me that needle I had so dearly wanted to avoid taking but now needed so the pain could be taken away and I could get through this.

It was smooth sailing after this point. I'd called my mum back after what I imagined was me hanging up on her mid contraction. The midwife swapped shifts, and I was gifted Abby, the loveliest British midwife who had compassion by the bucketload and made it feel like I had a friend by my side. They kept my meds topped way up, and I spent the next few hours talking to my family on the phone and keeping Craig informed via text, until he landed in Bali.

Eventually, my phone began to ring and I could see it was Craig. I answered with a simple 'hello' like it was just a normal day. I heard the panic in his voice, but by this point I was as sedated as I possibly could ever be, and my drawl must have soothed him. He proceeded to head back to the gate, and I could hear him telling the flight attendants, 'My fiancée is having a baby. I need to get back to Hong Kong now!' He ended up being able to get back on that same plane for its return to Hong Kong, and I wondered, being five hours away from Hong Kong, and a good extra hour to get to the hospital from the airport, if he'd make it.

I was more than happy to continue my labour pain-free and I even ordered a club sandwich from the hospital menu, after being advised to do so by the midwife, to give me energy for the next little bit. I was still talking to my mum and my sister regularly via text, but they both to went to sleep, as they were three hours in front of Hong Kong. I was also posting and replying to comments on Instagram, and managing the page. We were right in the middle of peak Spring Break season for the US, and our page needed constant attention, so I had no choice but to continue working as much as I could, which wasn't too bad in terms of keeping my mind off what was going on. Labour was moving slowly, and I felt confident I'd be still in the exact same position when Craig arrived.

My obstetrician was there with me the whole time, something I didn't realise at the time was usual practice after hours. He sat with me for a good hour, asking for my life story, and basically keeping me company.

Abby, my midwife, returned at about 9 pm and seemed a little perplexed as to my very slow-moving labour. She asked if I'd been to the toilet in the last few hours, and no, I hadn't. I couldn't even move my legs, thanks to the epidural, which I assume was topped up more often than usual to keep me feeling calm without having a support person there.

She inserted a catheter and my bladder emptied, which inadvertently expedited my labour, and five minutes later it was time to push.

The emotion of doing this alone had been stifled due to the epidural, but I still felt too scared to push, too reluctant to have this moment without Craig there. Again, my OB came through with the voice of reason. 'You're not alone – we're doing this together,' he said, and along with Abby the midwife there for support, I gave birth to Oscar Ellis, weighing a mere 2.4 kilograms, at 9.16pm on 1 April 2015. Yes, my firstborn was an April Fool's baby, pranking us by turning up five-and-a-half weeks early.

I was high, for lack of a better word, when they first placed him on my chest, and didn't even notice his little gasps for breath and pained sounds. I assumed that was how all newborns sounded! He was swiftly removed from me and placed on the little workbench while doctors came and went from the room in a rush, all things that I assumed were standard practice. I even spoke to Craig as he landed in Hong Kong, only minutes after the birth. I had answered the phone as Oscar was letting out one of his first big cries, which was a very bittersweet moment for Craig and me.

The minutes between that call and Craig arriving were a bit of a blur. I was fed some toast and given some tea, and told that Oscar wasn't breathing as well as they hoped and would be moved downstairs for more observations. I was totally unaware that he was being moved to intensive care because they'd worded it all so delicately, so that when Craig did eventually burst into the room, I calmly and quite happily told him Oscar was just in another room being monitored.

Of course, it was then that we were told Oscar was unwell and was unable to breathe unassisted.

The stark reality of this realisation sent my entire body cold, and what followed was twenty-four hours of complete hell. As soon as I was able to, I was taken down by wheelchair to Oscar's little pod. He was covered in tubes. I had a sick baby. And I just felt, in my gut, it was because of me. Because I'd been a sick adult. Because I'd weighed less at the end of my pregnancy, baby included, than I did at the start. Because I valued myself over my son's life. Because I couldn't put anyone before my stupid obsession with my weight.

It was all too much to process, and again these thoughts were pushed far down into the depths of my heart. Another burden to take on, to make me feel completely unworthy of anything good that was in my life.

It was a wild few days that came next, but with a course of antibiotics, Oscar showed up as the strong, healthy boy he has been since. The way he reacted to the antibiotics was something the doctors hadn't seen before. They told us it would be ten to twelve hours before we'd see any improvement, and I had returned to my hospital room to shower when not even twenty minutes later the midwife burst into the bathroom. 'Erin you have to come see this!' she said, and I rushed downstairs to find Oscar out of the pod, breathing alone, not even an hour after the antibiotics were first administered. His recovery was so swift, and so impressive, we left the hospital within the standard four days, now a family of three.

~

Life continued to move swiftly once we returned home to our apartment.

I worked straight through this post-partum period, without even any thought that it would be any other way. I was still replying to emails and posting on Instagram without a noticeable break (we were posting on our page numerous times a day at this point). But I didn't mind, at the time, at all. Having a baby felt like the most perfect gift, as exhausting as it was, and gave me a feeling of purpose and contentment I hadn't felt in a while. I was with Oscar 24/7, with occasional breaks between feeds when Craig would take him out for a walk so I could rest. I never was able to nap, even at my most exhausted moments! But it was all so special, and a time I still cherish. Craig had expressed his desire to be a parent from our very first date and was at ease with his role as a dad. He softened towards me noticeably during the time as well, which made me feel such ease at being a new mum. I had no expectations of how it would feel to be a mum, and I just remember feeling in absolute awe over him. We were alone, the three of us, with total stillness, to enjoy Oscar and have no one else insert themselves into our newborn bubble at all. I remember the firsts so clearly. The first time we went for a walk, the first time I sat at lunch, the first bath. It moved slowly and blissfully, and I will always cherish those weeks with nothing else and no one else to interrupt our time.

My weight plummeted, not even very consciously, and at one point, a few weeks after birth, I was down to my lowest ever weight, 48 kilograms. I am 180 centimetres tall, and my healthy weight is usually around the 65-kilogram mark. I'd always taken the smallest opportunity to stay lean, and knowing the post-partum period was depleting, went to the extreme of not compensating through food for all the nutrients I was losing, as only my mental illness knew how to do so well. Again, the fact I was overseas away from family and friends was how I was able to indulge in these behaviours, although perhaps if they had been around it wouldn't have made a difference anyway. My default setting was to restrict food at all times, regardless of any logic or external circumstances. Craig was very aware of my challenges at this time, but like with anyone who ever questioned my eating disorder throughout the years I battled with it, I would fly into a rage if ever questioned over it. My weight never fluctuated wildly, as I have always been lean and so perhaps it wasn't as obvious to those around me. I was extremely clever at manipulating mealtimes and situations where I had to eat in front of others, and it was rare anyone would have witnessed behaviours that were obviously disordered, even with Craig.

With all the busyness of work and life, Oscar felt like my safe space, where I was able to be calm, present and good at something. And I was a good mum. I was attentive, always there for him, always knowing what to do and when to do it.

When I say busyness, I really mean busyness! Months earlier, Craig and I had decided we wanted to leave Hong Kong. While we loved the city so much – and it had given us so many special times, largely tied to the business, but also just the energy of the city, and the simple times we spent going out for a meal, or going shopping together, or just walking around – we knew it wasn't the perfect place to raise children (pollution, lack of open space, green grass, etc), and so we'd spent a few months deliberating on where it was we were going to be based out of next.

The frontrunners were New York, London and Monaco.

New York was an obvious choice due to our market being predominantly in the US, but it was very complicated to live there in terms of visas, and taxes were high.

London was another possible choice but the summer was too short, and the long winters felt too miserable.

We decided on Monaco, a city I'd visited only once before, back in 2014, when we were invited by Sir Philip Green, founder of Topshop, to meet him and discuss potential investor opportunities for Triangl. A whirlwind twenty-four hours, resulting in a lunch on his superyacht, was an intoxicating introduction to Monaco, a small country town of billionaires, as I like to fondly call it. The appeal of Monaco for us, aside from it being a beautiful town on the French Riviera, was the favourable and well-known tax perk of 0 per cent personal tax.

Craig had gone all out in finding an apartment for us in Monaco, arranging furniture, cars – all of it. I won't dance around the fact that the tax scenario was appealing, and absolutely this played into our decision to live there, but we also fell in love with the idea of being in the heart of Europe. A three-hour drive from Milan, a two-hour drive from Saint-Tropez, a one-hour flight to Paris, two hours to London.

We also already felt like global citizens. Our lives were very much taking place on the road, and we were never anywhere for very long, already, by this point (little did I know how much more travel was to come!). Our business was purely online; it was purely on our laptops, on our phones. So we were really able to cherry-pick any kind of base we wanted to.

It was more of a 'why not' scenario with Monaco. Why not pay no tax? Especially when we were not often at home.

Our business also hadn't directly come from Australia, as such; we weren't an Australian brand. Our business was founded in Hong Kong. So we didn't feel like we belonged anywhere, which made us feel like Monaco might work. It also just felt so dream-like.

I would again be moving to a city I knew very little about, and it was exciting all over again, and hopeful all over again, and perhaps I was naive all over again, expecting this move to make me feel content finally. The difference in this move was that I hoped living in Monaco would somehow be an internal acknowledgement of the success Craig and I had had so far, and that we'd continue living 'the dream', which I was so desperately trying to convince myself I was living.

~

We had a few work trips arranged before the move, and after securing an emergency passport for Oscar, we were on our very first overseas trip as a family, back to Australia, to introduce our son to our relatives and friends and to collect his full passport. He was only one month old, and it was a very quick few days of introducing him to our family and a few friends. From there, we flew directly to LA, to meet with a PR agency, Bollare.

So far, we'd tried to avoid external PR agencies. Often they asked for big monthly retainers, and we never felt we saw any traction even remotely comparable to what we were getting ourselves so never really entertained the idea of them after the initial meeting. This worked totally fine in Australia, as we had a list of editors who we reached out to directly when and if we needed to release a new campaign via the press. The same logic applied to the UK and Europe; however, the United States, we quickly learned, was a different kettle of fish completely. While we had, and would continue to have, unbelievable growth and cut-through in the US, we knew that it was a place that was heavily celebrity-centric, and the way they were pretty much always reached out to was via showrooms that the agencies had. (All agencies are built around a showroom, where your brand offering is laid out for all guests to see. This is especially important in America, because this is where the celebrity stylists go, and so it's a very clear way for brands to reach all the celebrities, consistently.) Yes, we had had our Kendall Jenner moment, and many others, but we didn't think it was smart to feel we were above the way the system ran over there, so we visited a few LA agencies to see who might be the right fit.

While the bigger agencies were in New York, we felt the LA market was more where we needed to be based from in the US, with its celebrity dominance and being a beach city, which made more sense for a bikini brand. The funny thing was, it was around this time, we saw New York take over as being the strongest state in terms of bikini sales for Triangl, and this didn't change throughout the entire time I was running Triangl. However, it still felt that LA was a more natural fit as a state for us, so that's why we went with a showroom there, managed by a lovely bunch of younger women, the perfect representation of a Triangl customer.

We chose them to represent our brand. We wanted our positioning to be strong, so not only did we ensure our swimwear would be displayed well, but we made every effort to get to know everyone in the team. We gifted everyone in the office Triangl bikinis, and we knew that gesture would continue the buzz around the brand and put us in the best position to be spoken of highly when it came to showroom visits by stylists and also gifting suites, which were activations held by the agency before events like Coachella, Spring Break or Miami Swim Week, which were basically events where your bikinis were displayed on racks and models, to give your brand accessibility and visibility to celebrities and influencers.

It also really helped being a brand owned by Australians in the US, and having that really laidback Aussie vibe. It was a bit of a superpower of ours when we met with anyone in the States or in the UK. That Australian twang was a real novelty to Americans. They delighted in hearing the accent alone, not to mention the way we both spoke, which was definitely filled with lots of 'no worries', 'nah, all goods' and 'see ya later'! It certainly also helped that we had Oscar with us, at every single meeting. He came with us everywhere, and definitely added to our cool factor!

After Los Angeles, we visited Palm Springs, to scout some locations for upcoming photoshoots. Being only a two-hour drive from Los Angeles, we had hired a beautiful old Rolls-Royce for the trip. The only issue was securing a newborn car seat into the back of this very old prestige car. Which we, as brand-new parents, had not for one second considered. We had to fashion the seatbelts around the seat, and I ended up holding Oscar in the backseat for the majority of the car trips, as it felt safer than having him in a car seat that wasn't very well secured.

It was outrageously hot in Palm Springs on this trip, stinking hot. Essentially, Palm Springs is in the desert, so while the mornings and nights were cool, the daytime heat was not enjoyable, nor very safe for a newborn baby, and I stayed inside for the majority of those few days with Oscar. I clearly remember this trip being the first time that I really started to feel exhausted and quite fragile after having Oscar. He was an unsettled baby and seemed to hate most the stillness of nights when we wanted to get some sleep. Craig, one of those fortunate people who could just fall and stay asleep, never seemed to even twitch at the regular, endless wake-ups I endured during the nights, something I so clearly remember from this trip.

Perhaps it was the fact I'd been stuck in the hotel all day long, or that the adrenaline of the newborn bubble phase was well and truly over, but those nights felt torturous, lonely and very silent – the kind of silence that felt so bloody loud. Not even this gorgeous hotel suite we were in made a wink of difference; not even the fact we were moving to Monaco in mere days was helping. I felt total dread, total helplessness, total isolation and total shame over all these feelings.

Every night during this trip I promised myself I'd tell Craig when he woke how I was feeling, how scary these thoughts were. But as the sun rose every morning, and the light started to hit the corners of the curtains, that little glimmer of sun felt like a glimmer of hope.

Oscar was almost always sleeping peacefully next to me during the sunrise, as he always did in those early mornings, and I'd feel like I'd be able to get through another day and find a way to love this life I had.

~

From Palm Springs to LA and back to Hong Kong, the three of us arrived home to our apartment to pack up as quickly as we could because in two days we would be on a plane to our new home in Monaco. Packing up our Hong Kong life was easy enough, and aside from a few pieces of baby furniture, we had only our clothes to pack. Relying on the concierge from our Hong Kong apartment to assist in arranging the particulars, we left for our new home, barely taking any time to farewell the city that had given me so much – where my son, Oscar, and my other baby, Triangl, were born.

The very first Triangl Instagram post, because what became the business page used to be my personal page. It's my bedroom wall in the share house I lived in when I met Craig, in October 2011. The post is still up!

Unpacking the very first delivery of bikinis to Melbourne, in December 2012. These were the nylon/spandex styles, and I remember feeling so proud and excited to finally have physical products.

Craig in our first apartment in Hong Kong, in October 2012, before it became our office, warehouse and studio as well.

Me modelling our first collection on a beach in Hong Kong in late 2012. This was not something I enjoyed doing, and I much preferred when we could afford to use real models. I never felt thin enough, or pretty enough, to be photographed.

The living room of my family home in January 2013. I spent three sixteen-hour days ironing flat every single neoprene bikini that had arrived from our factory in China completely squashed.

A view of Hong Kong at night. The skyline was always so colourful and made me feel like I was never alone.

A behind-the-scenes image from my favourite ever Triangl shoot, which we shot in Sardinia from our superyacht in 2016.

Our very first #trianglgirl, Chloe. In fact, we named our first bikini style Chloe in honour of her.

The selection of bikinis we famously gifted Kendall Jenner in 2013, which she tweeted about to her five million followers, causing our brand to rocket into the US market.

Craig, Oscar and me in Spain in 2016, on the back of our superyacht *Neoprene* before we painted her matte black. A Mangusta 108, she was a sleek, unassuming but beautiful boat.

While these times were pretty special, I would always struggle greatly with my body image, lack of identity and loss of purpose during these trips.

Craig and me at La Fontelina in Capri, Italy, in August 2017. I was five months pregnant with Oly and we were there for a Triangl photoshoot.

A view of Port Hercules in Monaco where we moved in 2015. After having lived in Hong Kong, where a sunny day meant brighter pollution haze, the sun and sea in Monaco felt almost too good to be true. Image credit: Victor He, Unsplash

The view from the living room of our second apartment in Monaco. We moved into this place in mid-2017. It was a dreamy location and a beautiful villa-style home in the heart of Monte Carlo. In spite of all this beauty, Craig and I were heading quickly towards a separation as I was increasingly disconnecting from life around me.

The Christmas Day table setting from our apartment in Monaco in 2015. A private chef is in the background.

Having a snooze with Oscar just weeks before I gave birth to Oly. I remember feeling so contemplative about having another baby – like it meant I was somehow abandoning Oscar. Craig and I had only very recently separated and I was feeling very uncertain about my future and what was to come.

Oscar and Oly sleeping in my bed in New York in January 2018. The boys hadn't spent much time together since Oly was born (Oscar was more often with Craig). They started bonding when we moved to New York and, as a newly single mum, I felt hopeful and motivated to keep going for them. This wasn't to last though, as everything came crashing down around me that year.

Zac and me on our first holiday together in Hawaii in April 2019. It's hard to put into words how much I already loved Zac by this point. I honestly felt like I was in a dream when we were together – I was completely and totally smitten.

My first little girl, Beatrice, born in June 2020 – smack bang in the middle of the Covid pandemic. We weren't allowed any visitors in the hospital, which was a very relaxing experience.

Introducing Bobby, born in October 2021, to his older brothers and sister for the first time.

The Deering-Ellis-Keane family in January 2022

Chapter Nine

Private Jets and Superyachts

Monaco is truly the most unique place in the entire world I've ever visited, let alone lived in. I still find it complex beyond belief, to this day. Monaco is a well-documented 'tax haven', but it truly is in one of the most picturesque parts of the world as well. You are screened and checked prior to becoming Monégasque (and by screened I mean criminally and financially to ensure your criminal record doesn't exist and that your bank account is large enough) and once you secure that Identity Card, you still feel completely displaced, due to the transient, touristy nature of the entire place.

Our apartment was right on the border of France and Monaco, quite literally sticking your hand out our window would mean you were in France. It was a quieter part of Monaco; which perhaps wasn't the best thing, seeing as Monaco's life force was the fact it was always bustling with tourists and people coming and going. The apartment was old, but absolutely beautiful, with views directly out to the Mediterranean. A surreal realisation, indeed, that the most coveted ocean in the world was the one we were now suddenly looking out at, every day.

We were fortunate in the fact we rented an apartment that was fully furnished, albeit only temporarily until our replacement furniture, currently on order from, primarily, Italy, arrived. We knew that when we arrived, we'd be moving into a home with a dining table, couches and a bed – at the very least. When we both first laid eyes on the apartment the morning of our arrival, we immediately fell in love with the space, and while the furniture was not really our aesthetic, it was entirely livable, until all the new, more modern, furniture Craig had organised beforehand was delivered.

It also didn't really matter about the very dark, very ornate furniture because we only had one night in Monaco before we were to fly out to a board meeting. Our very first one actually, as we had recently set up our company in the Channel Islands, having no need to keep the company in Hong Kong now we had left. We had a supply chain office still in Hong Kong, but the creative was coming from us, and so we chose a base near us to suit, to coincide with our move to Europe. It meant our first night in our new home was overshadowed by work. Our few busy weeks prior to arrival had meant we'd been fallen a little behind on Triangl operations, and, as a result, we'd completely missed that a new collection of swimwear was in the warehouse ready to be sold. The only issue was it hadn't been uploaded yet online. The product had already been photographed on a mannequin for our still product images, and the photoshoot had been completed but we still needed to not only upload the styles on to the website but photoshop the mannequin out of the images to present them online in the way all our other products were displayed.

This process was one that Craig and I used to do from start to finish without fail, for every single collection release. However, Craig had long since handed over the photography and photoshop elements of the bikini uploading process, but the actual uploading of the product on to the website was still my job, as we felt it was too important to be left to anyone else.

That night, as Craig worked on the images, I began to set up the uploads. We had about twelve styles, so usually this task would take two to three hours in total. However, the issue was our internet. We had nothing set up in the apartment as yet, so we were tethering off our phones and the process was painstakingly slow. We'd committed to uploading the styles before we left the next day, and while there was nothing really relying on it, missing a day's sales, even when we were selling well over US$100,000 worth of bikinis a day, wasn't an option. So, for the first time in Triangl's history, we stayed up all night. At the time, I didn't think too much of it; after all, I was regularly up with Oscar and didn't feel it would be much different. But there's a certain psychology in preparing for bed, and getting into bed for the night, even if you don't sleep much, and missing that felt like a hardcore experience! When the sun had long risen, we were finally done. After a shower and change of clothes, we headed to the airport, for yet another 'first' – our first time flying on a private jet.

Both Craig and I were in a state of flux, going from exhausted, to exhilarated, to happy, to flat, but we were excited for this next big moment. It wasn't a bucket-list moment for me – I'd never dreamed of flying private, nor did I ever think I ever would – but it felt very cool to reach this unexpected milestone, a milestone that was most definitely reserved, in my eyes, for the ultra wealthy. Granted, it was much easier to fly private in Monaco. Flight times were short (we weren't flying to the USA, or back home to Australia, which would have cost six figures at least). And the access to private jets was fairly straightforward. We flew private only when it made sense logistically, for example – if we'd flown commercially for this board meeting, we'd have had to fly from Nice to London, and then back down to Jersey. The private option meant it was a direct flight to Jersey, which cut the travel time down significantly. Both a fancy and logistically smart option.

Growing up, we'd flown first-class domestic, back in the 1990s when there was a first class for domestic flights, which was entirely due to my dad's work in an insurance company, not our own family wealth. As an adult, it was economy all the way and I never ever imagined I'd ever get to fly at the pointy end of the plane. Our first business-class flight, to New York, not long after Triangl experienced its first taste of success through regular and continually growing bikini sales, is a very strong memory. Craig and I had laboured over the decision of whether to upgrade to business-class tickets now that we were doing so well financially. We knew it was a huge step up for us, and one we didn't want to do before we were really ready. Not only was the actual cost a huge jump from economy to business, but it wasn't something we were going to do once and then fly economy again the next time. It was signifying a pretty big lifestyle change for us, cementing our position as being wealthy enough to afford to fly business all the time, which was such a change to how we'd been merely a year prior to that moment. To now be in a position to fly on a private jet felt almost comical. Often these big-ticket moments felt dream-like. I often felt detached from the moments themselves; perhaps it was a bit of self-preservation. It always felt a bit silly, like we were about to get caught for faking it.

The private airport in Nice was very standard. Nothing opulent or fancy, although I hadn't been too sure what to expect, anyway. There were small lounges and waiting rooms, but there didn't seem to be much need for these, given private planes don't usually require long waits, unless there are sudden weather changes. Once we had been through security, we were ushered into a white Mercedes people mover, which drove us past the longest line of private planes I'd ever seen, likely owned by some of the wealthiest people in the world.

Driving past these planes felt completely surreal; it was a side of life I'd never thought I'd really see up close like this, let alone be a part of. I naively assumed all private planes to be of the same size, but to find them all so different was such a shock to me. Some were the size of a Boeing 767, and some were fairly small. The further we drove down the tarmac, the smaller the planes got, and I was hopeful we were going to still have something decent enough to feel exciting after seeing these huge jets. I won't lie, I was underwhelmed and a little bit disappointed to pull up to our tiny little jet, which looked a lot more like a prop plane. But, hey, we were flying private, and it was going to be a momentous occasion nonetheless!

We met the captain and co-captain outside the plane, and climbed in. Cockpit to the left, a small four seats to the right, and a tiny little toilet behind that. The plane was so small neither of us could fully stand up in it, so we took our seats and both tried to take the moment in. I was expecting, or just hoping, for a glass of champagne, a toast to our first private plane experience! But there was only a bottle of water in each armrest and a little basket of Trolli gummy worm packets to celebrate with.

With the gloss well and truly taken off, the plane taxied down the runway and took off. This was very cool, as I'd never been in a light plane before, and the speed with which the plane took off was a total surprise. We were in the clouds in a fraction of the time it would take a commercial plane, and the efficiency of flying private was obvious in that moment.

Oscar slept the whole time, sandwiched in the aisle between our seats. Craig and I both fell immediately asleep as well, although mine felt more of a doze, considering we were sitting bolt upright in our seats.

Once we landed, we went straight to our board meeting, the first of its kind for Triangl and for Craig and me as directors. It didn't take long for the lack of sleep to present itself. There were four of us in the boardroom, me, Craig, our CFO, John, and our director of the UK company, Lindsay. John was an Australian, living in Monaco, the brother-in-law of one of Craig's best friends from Melbourne, and Lindsay lived in Jersey, and was hired to run the operations there. The delirium of no sleep was taking hold, and combined with a stuffy, windowless boardroom, it didn't take long before things took a turn for the worse. A comment was made, something harmless and pointless, something so small I cannot to this day even recall it, but it sent both Craig and me into absolute hysterics. The kind of laugh you know you can't do, which therefore makes you want to do it more. Every time we tried to stop, the absurdity of the whole situation would hit, and we'd start laughing again. This kind of laugh was the one where tears stream from your eyes, and everything shakes; the laugh in which every part of your mind is willing you to stop but your body has other plans. We would have looked like two completely insane people, laughing uncontrollably for a good fifteen minutes. I recall feeling mildly embarrassed at our lack of professionalism, but also – because essentially we were the bosses, no one said anything, or even encouraged us to take a break – I guess it was up to us to call a little reset, due to us being the ones holding a meeting. But, to me anyway, those moments felt like a true experience of how much I was playing pretend. Pretending to be this big company owner and adult, when, really, I was still a young girl trying to trick everyone into thinking I was capable of sitting with the grownups.

The whole experience was absurd. Surreal. Out of body. It was all too much for me that day, and we flew back home that afternoon, grateful to be met by the silence of the old furniture in our new apartment, to not be around anyone. I just wanted to be 'home' after those kinds of workdays, wherever 'home' was, with Oscar, in silence, because it was there I didn't have to show up and act like I knew what I was doing.

~

We flew straight to the Maldives for a photoshoot the very next day. We hadn't even seen Monaco yet, or had a moment to settle, but business was business, and the shoots took priority always. This photoshoot, like all the photoshoots, was coordinated by me. Booking models, photographer, hair, makeup, arranging flights, accommodation, transfers – all of the logistics. A full-time role in itself and definitely not one of my favourite things to do, given modelling agencies loved to fight over day rates, and their numerous add-ons, for agency fees, travel fees, 'whatever else they could think of' fees. It was always a battle when requesting a certain model for a shoot. The agency would ask for our budget, which I never knew, as I didn't know what the day rate was for this model. The reason they asked was to ascertain how much we'd be willing to pay. We, being from Triangl, would get quoted astronomical day rates, because they knew we 'could' pay for it. The back and forth to get prices down was exhausting and also mildly satisfying when I'd eventually get a rate which was more in line with standard industry rates (which I knew from my experience with other models and businesses prior to Triangl), and without the 50 per cent mark up just for being a successful brand.

I had planned this particular shoot during the course of the last month, from the time Oscar was two weeks old, and at the time it all felt reasonably achievable – to work while caring for Oscar. His routine of feed, burp, nurse, sleep and repeat was quite easy to manage across time zones, and juggling work in-between it all felt doable. I felt I was experiencing a normal level of exhaustion for a new mum, and that it would be similar to the tiredness other new mums would be feeling. And perhaps this was true, but I was in the minority of mums changing time zones every few days while largely running the operations of a multi-million-dollar swimwear label.

The Maldives, admittedly, was a beautiful place to be with a new baby. It was the first time we had been to this island country, and it was every bit as picturesque as photos make it out to be. As tended to be the way with our photoshoots, we were combining a holiday with work, and we always had a few days either side of the shoot schedule to settle in, relax and enjoy the surroundings.

We also designed our schedule to be this way to ensure we had a few solid days of sun, as tropical locations are renowned for cloudy, rainy, stormy days and we wanted to ensure we didn't have to be forced to shoot on one of those.

We had a beautiful villa on the beach and I welcomed the breastfeeding breaks I got to have with Oscar, the opportunity every two to three hours to go into the air-conditioned room and sit in stillness with him. Oscar was a quick feeder, and, by then, easy to settle and put to sleep. He caused me no stress at any point during these early months, and I think it was because I so enjoyed being there for him 24/7. I breastfed Oscar for almost two years, exclusively. No bottle, no expressing, no breaks. I was there every three hours for him until I finally weaned him just weeks shy of his second birthday.

It was just after this time in the Maldives that I began to experience frequent bouts of illness. What I came to learn, after asking my mum back in Australia, was that I was getting some form of mastitis. I had extremely high fevers, body chills, migraines, nausea, complete exhaustion and fatigue. At its peak this was occurring every week, and always every few weeks throughout the entirety of my two-year breastfeeding journey with Oscar. I was in such martyr mode in the sense of neglecting myself, and focusing only on Oscar and Triangl, that I would just ride each episode out, without any attempt to further understand why it was recurring so regularly. I would still function as if I was fully healthy and well, as we often were in another location when a bout would hit. Each episode would last for twenty-four to forty-eight hours, and it would start suddenly, within an hour, with the same effects of blurry vision, rush of heat in my body and pounding headache, localised to a spot in my head that always made it very clear what was to come. An illness, I am sure, I could have had help with overcoming; however, I didn't have a doctor or know of one in Monaco, and we travelled so frequently during this time that I just didn't make it a priority to seek any help.

Oscar came with us everywhere in our early years as parents. And I mean everywhere. To every meeting, every dinner, every office visit, to every hotel, on every flight. He'd visited so many countries in his first year of life that I stopped counting. Oscar's only version of home was me. I was his absolute lifeline to security, consistency, structure and safety. I was always there. He slept in our bed, he napped by my side. He was with me always. He became my life force, my reason for existing, my purpose, and he brought me a lot of joy in a time I struggled to find anything fulfilling on a deeper level.

I often relied on these times with Oscar, tending to him, to take me away from the chaos of Triangl life, and my life in general. I would feel so much shame about wanting to get away from the business at all times, and mentally torture myself over the fact I was so resentful towards something that gave me so much. I just wanted to be alone, in my own space, with Oscar. I wanted quiet, I wanted calm. I so deeply wanted to hear nothing and feel nothing. But my mind would never stop with the thoughts, the chaotic thoughts, fuelled by complete exhaustion and sleep deprivation, that seemingly never ended – centred around how I didn't want to be here, I didn't want this life, but without knowing where I wanted to be instead. These thoughts caused a level of desolation in me I didn't know how to control, let alone even begin to process.

There was nowhere to go, no one to talk to, nothing to do other than shove the thoughts back into my mind and head back into the real world.

~

After the Maldives, we returned to Monaco for a short time to get acquainted with our new home. We had moved to Monaco at a really lovely time. It was high summer – blue skies and sunshine every single day. We slowly integrated ourselves into our home. Monaco is geographically small, and initially we found it very complex to understand. Firstly, it's a French-speaking place, and we found the French had a certain attitude to life that didn't lend itself well to our bumbling, laidback, loud Australian ways. My usual overly chirpy, chatty demeanour was not met with the kind of appreciation it was back in Australia, Hong Kong or the US (where Aussie slang is somewhat revered). The French quite simply came across as very rude to me, and while I spent many months initially trying to win them over with kindness, and with my supposed 'Aussie charm', I eventually found success in assimilating to their way of interacting, which

146

to me felt quite rude, but was considered by the French as direct, confident and clear. The practice of maintaining the French 'way' was one I took a very long time to get on board with.

We did try to learn French when we moved to Monaco. We had private lessons and started with a bang; however, as we spent the majority of the second half of 2015 travelling, any consistency to our learning was thwarted, and once enough time had passed for us to consider Monaco our home base, we'd become adept at managing in English, along with the French phrases and short sentences required by any foreigners who live in a French-speaking city.

The constant travel didn't just impact our ability to learn French, but really any other consistent routine that I ever tried to implement. I was starting to become interested in exercise, namely Pilates, and I'd found a clinical Pilates studio to teach me the foundational moves and exercises. However, it was stop–start to say the least, and it became such a challenge to find time to make the classes at all, let alone get any kind of consistency with them. The same happened with yoga, a practice that to this day I so dearly want to absorb into my life, but had absolutely no opportunity to back then, considering we were on the move so often.

Our constant travel for work also impacted on our ability to forge any relationships at all in Monaco. It was already a fairly impossible task to make friends in this city due to the language and cultural barriers (other than those who had been born in Monaco, it was mainly made up of Russian, French, Italian and English residents) but combined with the fact we were rarely home for more than two weeks at a time, it was easier to just stay in our own bubble.

Fortunately for me, I did have Chantal. We'd brought in another designer to assist Craig not long before we moved to Monaco, and she came with us to live in the city. She was Australian and had worked with Craig in his previous role in Melbourne. We became close immediately. We were together every day working, and, on weekends we would hang out in Monaco, either at the beach or beach club, with Oscar in tow always.

Without Chantal's company, my mental health would have plummeted so far, and so fast, I would not have lasted the years I did in Monaco, but, thanks to her, I had someone to spend my free time with, someone I could actually call a friend. Aside from Craig, I had no one to spend any of my time with, let alone another woman who was into fashion, eating well and enjoying a cocktail every now and again. Chantal was effectively an employee of the company, but she was so much more than that to me, and she was there for me in times of great personal need.

Even with Chantal's company, I still craved more connection, more routine, more structure. Sometimes it isn't until you try something that you realise it isn't what you want, and, for me, this constant up-and-go lifestyle, this nomadic way of living, was absolutely not how I wanted to live. But because it was 'the dream', and we were visiting the most beautiful places in the world, I sucked it up and held it in, but so badly longed for normality – just really to be in one place for a decent period of time.

We found Monaco, when we actually got to be there, absolutely beautiful, and its proximity to other desirable places made it even more special. We'd bought a car almost as soon as we'd arrived. A Range Rover, which was a car we both had always wanted to own. It was perhaps a little too big for the extremely narrow roads in Monaco and the even smaller car parks (I would often have to climb out of the passenger side door after parking in an underground car park in Monaco – so glamorous – but it fit a car seat in the back easily and also luggage for our weekends away in

Milan or Saint-Tropez). It wasn't hard to find cars in Monaco, especially prestige ones. While a car wasn't entirely necessary for Monaco itself – the entire principality can be walked around in an hour – to access the rest of France and Italy and beyond meant a car became a real asset to our life.

Our first trips were deep into the south of France. We'd already become familiar with Nice, as that's where the closest airport was and only a thirty-minute drive from Monaco. An extra thirty minutes and you were in Antibes, then Cannes, finishing up at Saint-Tropez.

It was my first time visiting this part of France, and it definitely had a different feel knowing this wasn't so much a holiday, but close to home. Admittedly I wasn't as enamoured with Saint-Tropez or Cannes as I had hoped to be; perhaps it was driving into the cities during peak summer season, where you were often stuck in standstill traffic for hours, or the influx of tourists, but they felt gimmicky and were not places I wanted to spend time in.

By the time we were able to begin to explore the other side of Monaco – Italy – we had our boat, which had arrived from Hong Kong. We probably had one of the smallest boats in Monaco, but with it we were able to make our first trips into Italy by sea rather than road, which initiated our love affair with the quaint coastal towns on the Italian coast and their way of life, which seemed slower, more intentional, more beautiful.

It didn't take long for us to think about buying a bigger boat, and we spent many months assessing and initiating ourselves into the market of superyachts, a whole new world of wealth and luxury that I'd never ever *ever* thought I'd find myself in. The dizziness associated with having money after none at all was something I had never navigated before and we definitely found it alluring to think of all the things we could suddenly purchase that had seemed completely off limits until now.

~

It wasn't long before Triangl snapped us back to reality. After all, we were still running a now-global business, with very few employees to rely on when we took the foot off the pedal. We found out our factory was struggling to keep up with the sheer volume of orders coming through. It was resulting in sold-out styles online, something we had never wanted to occur in our selling model – in fact, something we didn't have built into our model at all – so it was causing relative chaos in terms of stock management online and customer care, as well as the obvious manufacturing challenges.

We decided to head back to Hong Kong for a while to sort out the scaling challenges we were having. These challenges felt scarier than the startup issues of making sales because we had such a large customer base and were selling thousands of pairs a day, so the impact of errors like running out of stock were a lot bigger and required fast and diligent solutions, ones that were still completely up to Craig and me to solve at a managerial level.

Fortunately, we'd set up systems and structures which were straightforward in our eyes, and easy enough to course-correct with both Craig and me in the Hong Kong office, focusing on the business solely for a week or two. During these periods we worked closely alongside our supply chain team, who were amazing at running operations in our absence until something needed to be looked at with authority, in which case it was often ignored until it would, by total luck, be brought to our attention. It's how we ended up over ordering $1,000,000 worth of fabric over a two-year period. This oversight could have eventually destroyed the business, but thankfully we were able to use the fabric ongoing and stop future orders being placed indefinitely.

For that second half of 2015, and first half of 2016, we spent only a quarter of our time in Monaco, with the other three quarters split between Hong Kong and various other locations. We visited New York, Paris, London, Milan, Bali and the Maldives frequently, for a combination of work and play. We had become very good at being able to fit both elements into every trip we took.

We decided to spend Christmas 2015 in Monaco, which was a change from previous years where we'd always returned home to Melbourne. We extended an invite to both families to join us for a week at home. Craig's family was unable to make it, which did rather devastate Craig at the time. He was very close to his dad, and we were hoping they were able to come, but the trip was too far and they declined the invitation. Bree, my older sister, also shared the same sentiment as Craig's family (perhaps it was due to coming over our winter time), but my parents and younger brother, Myles, made the trip.

A photoshoot in the Maldives, and a few nights in London, and then, a couple of days shy of Christmas, Craig, Oscar and I arrived home to an apartment that we hadn't visited in over two months, now completely furnished and set up with all the items Craig had been ordering since we first planned our Monaco move, by our French assistant/sometime nanny, Isabelle.

After a solid six months of living in hotels and not really having anywhere we could call 'home', the feeling of finally having a place that looked and felt like ours to come home to was really comforting. We arrived back in Monaco at the same time my parents and brother landed from Melbourne, so they were seeing our newly furnished apartment almost at the same time as we were for the first time. I was so excited to have my family there and host them over Christmas.

I'd booked a dinner on Christmas Eve at the restaurant at Hotel Metropole, one of the best hotels in Monaco. This set the tone for a beautiful few days. In Europe, Christmas is largely celebrated on Christmas Eve, so the festive feels were very apparent. It felt really special to have my parents there, and to enjoy Oscar's first Christmas as a family. It was so often just Craig, Oscar and I – so to have other loved ones with us felt so important and just bloody lovely. On Christmas Day, we hosted a big lunch at home. For months leading up to this, I'd been thoroughly enjoying planning the event. We had a private chef booked from the Fairmont, one of the classic Monaco hotels. He cooked a three-course meal, and we also had waitstaff to ensure everyone was looked after. I'd transformed our dining table and surrounding spaces with incredible florals and greenery, and had a 2.1-metre-tall Christmas tree installed, with decorations a plenty. We served my favourite champagne (Ruinart Blanc de Blanc) and an array of incredible French white and red wines. We invited our CFO, John, and his wife, Kim. It was an absolutely perfect Christmas Day, and I felt really so proud to be able to host in this way. It is still a favourite memory of Monaco.

In the days that followed, Craig and I were able to showcase the very best of Monégasque life. We took helicopters to Saint-Tropez for lunch at Club 55; we took our boat out for a day trip to have lunch on the water. Both my parents were in awe of the life we'd created, and I have clear memories of my dad's repeated 'wows' and 'ahhs' at all the wild Monaco moments, and my mum often squeezing my arm to say, 'Darling, this is all so wonderful!' It was still as surreal for me as it was for them though. Not only when comparing it to how I grew up, in this middle-class family in Melbourne, but the comparison to our life in Hong Kong only a couple of years earlier. Through our incredibly hard work, our business had had a meteoric rise, and it was taking some time for the lifestyle this allowed us to have to feel in any way real. Seeing it through my family's eyes, who were so happy and proud of us, made me realise how my own emotions hadn't caught up to being able to accept the opulent life we were living as reality.

It was bittersweet saying goodbye, and I felt maybe even a little guilty that they were returning to their normal lives, and we were continuing our life of luxury and upwards trajectory to goodness knows where.

And we really were off again, only one day into the new year – heading straight to New York for the start of a very big few months for Triangl – and its future.

Chapter Ten

Is This Freedom?

Sometime during 2015, due to the sheer number of emails Craig and I would receive, asking if we were interested in selling our business, looking to take on investors, raise capital and so on, we began to entertain the idea of selling Triangl, whether it be a minority or majority share of the business.

What we had achieved, in such a short time, was something not many had seen before, and we had become a very hot brand, initially to the venture capitalists but more so to the private equity groups.

This part of a business and the growth of a business was the most unfamiliar experience I'd ever had. It was one thing to make customers happy and receive praise from the press, but to have big firms shaking their heads in disbelief at the genius of what we'd done felt so foreign to me, and was comical in so many ways.

Craig and I were by no means professional business people, and we'd be turning up to some of the largest private equity firms in the world in jeans, and, as always, I'd have Oscar with me, a six-month-old baby, sitting in a boardroom as we talked finances. It honestly made me want to burst out laughing at the sheer absurdity of it all. We had never done a business plan, we'd never planned for this. It felt like Triangl happened to us, rather than that we'd made it happen. And, in a way, this was true.

We had set out only wanting to sell one bikini a day. We didn't plan for this viral bikini, this global sensation, and while we were thrilled it went the way it did, we were never really able to articulate the reasons why it had.

It didn't take long for me to become obsessed with the idea of selling, of taking the money that was on the table for us. But what became even clearer to me was that I wanted more resources, more infrastructure. I wanted help. I wanted experts to come in and tell me what to do next.

I was so in over my head by this point and had no confidence or even desire to keep going at the rate I was. I also was exhausted by it all. I just wanted to stop for a while. And I knew I couldn't, so having others take the brand over to some capacity felt like the absolute best option for me to get a fucking break.

What we realised fairly quickly was that no one wanted to buy us outright, in a simple transaction. The business was only effectively two years old and lacking in infrastructure, so the business IP was largely wrapped up in Craig and me, and therefore we had to be part of the deal.

This left us with either a full sale, a five-year exit plan, a majority sale or a minority sale.

A majority sale was selling around 80 per cent of the business, with us keeping 20 per cent and only staying on in an advisory role of sorts. A minority sale was selling off anywhere from 10 to 40 per cent of the business, which meant we would stay in control but that we would be able bring in an investor or firm with a particular skill set to further drive Triangl's success.

This was when the valuations started rolling in. Valuations which really had no foundation other than the ones placed on the business by outsiders. These valuations were big, but they were thrown around without much care or consideration. This was when I learned how fragile the the private equity, big investment firm world is. It felt like numbers were always based on 'blue sky' expectations – based on the assumption that sales figures were only going to rise and profit margins would continue to be extremely strong – and I learned how risky it was to put those figures out into the world. Obviously we were still seduced by both these valuations and the huge potential we were being told Triangl had to take over the swimwear world and to dominate in other categories as well.

The amount of time Craig and I spent talking over these plans, these possibilities, questioning if we wanted Triangl, if we wanted investors, if we wanted money was all-consuming. We'd convince ourselves of one way forward, and would decide on a plan, only to then wake up the next day and change our minds. We'd never been in this situation before, and while we were guided exceptionally well by an Australian investment bank, who we had engaged to assist with the sale, the decision was very much up to us.

The most recurrent message that every potential firm would give us in their meetings when they were pitching to us was: 'We just want to do great things and have fun.' Their pitches and promises were supposed to be alluring, exciting, but I remember finding it so frightening. Where was this 'fun'? Triangl didn't feel like it had been very 'fun' for me.

It was all I had; it was all Craig had. It was an extension of the both of us. And while it was the most incredible time, for both good and bad reasons, it never felt 'fun'. Fun felt flippant. Fun felt dangerous. And it always made me very wary of these people in these boardrooms. What was a wrong investment for them would be the end of our professional lives for us. It wasn't their entire life's purpose, and yet it certainly felt like mine, and for it to be discussed in such casual terms rang clear and loud alarm bells for what they planned to do to Triangl, to us.

Additionally, in every discussion Craig and I had, every time we'd plan out what it meant to suddenly have US$100 million, and the things we could do, and where it would take us, we'd remind ourselves of how we were already doing more than we'd ever dreamed we could do, *and* we were doing it with total freedom, without anyone else dictating to us or weighing in on our decisions.

And that was always what grounded us, centred us, held us off making the decision for another day: that we'd started Triangl to have freedom. To not have a boss. To have autonomy over every decision we'd made. And selling even some of Triangl meant we'd lose that. And we both knew, deep down, that was never going to be an option. For months, though, we still came back to these meetings, these discussions – we felt we owed it to Triangl to see if we were able to take it further than we could alone.

But the decision always felt like it was made for us when we thought about our freedom. And while I was somewhat resentful of this because I didn't feel that free anyway within the business, it felt right to honour the biggest reason for starting our own business, and it felt good to know we were sticking with our values.

With all this talk of selling dominating the first six months of 2016, our focus slipped from Triangl, and, while we were keeping the brand running, we weren't doing much innovating or developing new ideas. We didn't really feel we needed to; this year had been exceeding expectations – every week we did better numbers than the last, and our personal wealth was at a level where we both fully stepped into the knowledge and realisation that we were not going to end up without money ever again. We were multi-millionaires.

Being able to afford everything we could ever have wanted was a little bit of a distraction. We looked to buy homes in almost all of our favourite cities, and I still fondly recall the beautiful SoHo loft we almost signed papers for in New York, and the apartment in Milan, which was once owned by Giorgio Armani, that we almost took possession of. Once we left the cities though, the desire to purchase these places subsided, and the reality of wondering if we'd ever use those places would set in. We settled for buying artwork often, which was a far less involved transaction, one being an Andy Warhol 'Marilyn', and another, a Roy Lichtenstein pop art piece. I was also still feverishly buying designer clothes and accessories whenever I got the chance, which was pretty much daily by this point.

The one thing we did decide to commit to was a superyacht. Something I'd never thought I'd ever stay on, let alone own. We'd had the most beautiful times on our smaller boat, which was a Sunseeker 60, and living in Monaco allowed easy access to parts of the world we knew would feel special on a boat. We knew we could afford to upgrade so, after months of searching, Craig found an Italian yacht, a Mangusta 108. It was 108 feet in length, with five bedrooms and an engine to rival a speedboat's. The plan was to shoot as many Triangl campaigns on it as we could, and therefore justify the decision to buy the superyacht as something that would benefit our work.

We stayed on the yacht, aptly named Neoprene, in the Mediterranean for the better part of three months, only breaking for a trip to Miami for a trade show. Miami Swim Week was the biggest week in the US for swimwear brands, and it was a big gifting/influencer opportunity for our PR agency in LA, as well as being a very large trade show for swimwear and resort wear brands.

We'd always had requests to start wholesaling, from what felt like every single retailer in the world. It was always a hard and fast no from us to wholesale, but we started to wonder if we were missing an opportunity by not utilising this distribution channel, an opportunity, as we saw, to perhaps fulfil our customers' needs better by having our bikinis even more readily available to them. When we had launched Triangl three years before, we'd initially started with a wholesale model because we wanted our customers to find our bikinis in the same places where they bought their favourite fashion pieces. However, we'd abandoned that model quickly as the appeal of ecommerce, and selling direct to the consumer, spoke more to us.

The Miami Swim Week trade show was a little PR move as well, as we'd always been so hidden away as a brand and an absolute mystery to everyone through our choice to stay online only, which in itself led to anonymity, so we felt it was time to show who we were, in a safe way.

Most stalls in the pavilion were a very standard setup. Some racks, a table and that was basically it. However, we wanted to do it differently. Bigger, if you will. After all, it was our first real introduction of our brand, directly, to anyone, that we'd done anywhere. Craig and I, outside of a few quotes to publications, had never directly done anything where we spoke of or about the brand, so this was a big moment for us.

We had negotiated the biggest space in the hall. And Craig had spent months meticulously designing a display set of walls, to merchandise the swimwear in a way that showed it off in the best way possible to launch at the trade show. We also brought over couches and chairs from Italy. The most high-end display perhaps this trade show had ever seen. It was absolutely flawless, and probably one of the proudest few days of my life, being able to see the brand in real life, in a way we'd never been able to show it before, direct to retailers and wholesalers.

Those few days were big. They were exhausting, but they were so affirming. Every person who walked into our space at the trade show had the same reaction. 'Oh my gosh, Triangl!' Everyone wanted to place orders, then and there. But of course, we had nothing prepared. No line sheets, no systems. Opening up the wholesale side of the business was something we weren't even completely sure we were going to do. So I took business cards. I took phone numbers and email addresses and promised to get in touch once we were ready to take on accounts.

By the end of the three days, I had hundreds of contacts. It was clear we'd have a successful wholesale system, but we needed to invest in it, we needed to hire a team, we needed to basically set up a new business to facilitate these hundreds of accounts. It would be a lot of work and I needed to get my head around what to do next.

~

We returned to the boat and went back to the life we'd become used to.

That didn't mean we weren't working, but we had no capacity to work on anything new. I could have driven a wholesale system, but I didn't know where to begin. I didn't know how to begin. I didn't have the drive or desire to start again with a model that would require a lot of input, basically requiring a whole team of sales managers to run. Those hundreds of business cards I'd been given at Miami Swim Week were never touched again. I never emailed a single person about wholesale, and we moved on as if it had never happened.

This was very much a common occurrence in the business by this point. Not much made it past the ideation phase, and, if it did, it was never followed through with. We just simply didn't have the resources to take on anything new, and for me specifically, I had no desire or ability to add to my workload at all.

My lack of passion, purpose, happiness and joy was becoming more obvious to not only myself, but to everyone around me, in my daily life. It was easy enough to put the shame and sadness aside when on the boat, as it was a truly beautiful experience. We had friends at times, from Australia, come and stay on the boat with us, and there were many happy times. It was only at night-time that I felt the enormity of what was going on in my mind, which was a chaotic ball of hateful, shameful feelings about not knowing who I was and why I couldn't just feel fulfilled in this incredible life I was living.

It was when we got back to our apartment in Monaco that the threads would really unravel. Craig and I would argue over everything, and while our differing points of view had been part of our dynamic since the very beginning of our relationship, I became unbelievably sensitive to everything being said. I was so deeply sleep-deprived and restricting my food intake as much as possible, so my emotions were in a state of constant flux.

I blamed everything around me for the way I felt, and was utterly disempowered to make any changes. The sheer rage I felt at myself for being this way caused me to start self-harming.

Quite often, after Craig and I would have a big argument, I would start to repeatedly punch myself in the head. I'd been doing this on and off for years, during really inflamed and big arguments. I remember one incidence of this so clearly, from back when we were in Hong Kong. I couldn't even tell you now what we were arguing about, but it took the same toxic path, one where I had no way to express my feelings or thoughts and certainly no way to rationalise them.

I would always start with the clenched fists, and I'd feel like I was trapped. It felt like I was a rat in a cage. I'd pace back and forth, taking small baby steps, trying to settle my thoughts, calm myself down, but I was so heightened with rage, it was not possible. Craig was not there at this point to me; he did not exist. I'd gone into my own world, my own hell. I'd grab my head with both hands, trying to squeeze it enough for the chaotic thoughts to stop, or slow down. That never worked, and so I'd sink to the ground and often with just one fist, my left, I'd punch myself over and over and over again. There is no logic to this behaviour, there is no explanation that I can think of, other than I wanted it all to stop. I wanted to be removed from where I was; I wanted to disappear. And this was the only way I felt I could disappear: if I knocked myself out. I never succeeded in doing so, but I often got very close.

My mind was in such a frenzy, and I had absolutely no tools or understanding of how to calm myself down and how to feel safe again, so I had to do something to stop it, and physically was the only way. The blinding headache that immediately followed would calm my emotional state, making me feel numb.

It was in those moments I questioned everything. I didn't want to live like this; I didn't want to live at all. Manic is the only way I could describe it. Causing myself physical pain, cuts in my head, lumps that stayed for days, despite jolting me out of the state I was in, perpetuated my despair of feeling this way, of being like this. And feeling so shameful as to how I was even here, still here, after all my success, after cultivating this 'dream life', held me back from seeking the help I so desperately needed.

I was so angry and so resentful, and I held on to those emotions rather than leaning into being vulnerable and honest, and it kept me from seeking anything – any help – that would actually make me feel better. I hated myself, I hated Craig, I hated Triangl; the only person I loved was Oscar, which was unhealthy in itself as I had built such a dependence on him to soothe my soul.

My relationship with Craig was incredibly fragile at this point, and the differences in who we were as people had become so obvious and detrimental to us that almost every interaction ended in an argument or disagreement. Craig was obsessed with work, obsessed with success, obsessed with whatever he felt passionate about. He was also incredibly direct, and it was usually me who was on the receiving end of his directness. I was always sensitive to this side of him, but it worsened over the years, and I took everything he said as a complete attack on who I was, most likely because I had no idea who I was, so the foundation wasn't hard to crack. By this stage, I despised him, and made no secret of how much I blamed him for every single woe I had. But, despite this, we spent December, and ultimately Christmas, in New York, perhaps in an effort to take us away from Monaco, which seemed to always be the place things were most fractious in our relationship, even though it was also a place where we'd shared wonderful times. We'd been in New York for a month in the previous winter during Winter Storm Jonas, the second biggest snowstorm the city had ever seen, which for us had been the most beautiful time for the three of us, hunkered down cosily together inside and unable to go anywhere, so recreating this feeling felt like it was worth a shot.

Within the first week of arriving, Craig became extremely unwell with the flu. I followed shortly after, and then Oscar. We'd rented a huge loft on Broadway and spent the first two weeks inside, very ill. It was a very cold December and our very warm apartment felt safe and cosy, even during our days of high fevers, chills and aches and pains.

We were all feeling much better come Christmas Day, and, with no plans, we decided to take the subway up to Central Park. It was a cold but sunny day, and New York felt even more magical than usual. We walked past one of our favourite restaurants, Harry Cipriani, on Fifth Avenue, and thought we'd check if they had any space at all. Surprisingly, they did, and we had a lovely lunch, just the three of us, followed by a walk in Central Park. Not even a bout of mastitis, which hit me hard in the middle of lunch, could spoil the day, and once we returned home, I took up refuge on the couch, while Craig prepared the Christmas dinner I'd half organised.

I remember this as one of the best Christmas Days I've ever had. While I was definitely suffering during this time in my life, it showed me that life wasn't always one way or the other. It wasn't always happy or sad; more often than not, those feelings occurred on the same day, same week, or same month. It was life, and it was just that mine was out of balance. But as yet, I had no idea how I would get some balance back.

Chapter Eleven

Unravelling

S pirituality and mindfulness – words I'd always paid minimal attention
to.

Craig had always had some interest in the space, and in fact it was one of
the main things I loved about him, how he always had this understanding
of the way life was supposed to be, and a trust in timing and the divineness
of things working out as they were always going to.

He was always introducing me to different practices for me to try, to
support me in feeling better. At times, I found it mildly helpful, and I
tried to get into the meditations and the teachings, but at my worst times
I resented him for even suggesting anything, as it felt like an attack in itself,
rather than the help it was intended to be.

Craig had introduced me to kinesiology well before I became reliant on
it, much later, for healing. We both committed to sessions, but I refused
to be honest – refused to go into the suffering I was feeling – and it made
for an unhelpful experience.

He had also been the one to suggest my Indian meditation retreat,
where I again gave very little and therefore took little away. My reluctance
to be honest and vulnerable, and share how I didn't want to be living this

life, could have saved me, would have saved me. But I didn't trust any of that, so I kept everything inside.

Craig had been following a spirituality practice for some time now, where the ethos was quite simply to 'let it go'. It was as simple as this, and was to stop you in the moment of feeling any fear, anger, worry, stress, sadness and so on – and let go of your suffering.

It was as simple and as complex as that. And one I could not at all get into.

I was, however, always willing to try these things, and with a retreat being hosted in Sedona, Arizona, over New Year's Eve of 2016, we booked to go.

In Sedona, a city renowned for its spirituality and wellness, we were staying in a very standard hotel, nothing fancy, but it felt right for a three-day wellness retreat, as it was not about the high life.

For me, the retreat turned out to be the biggest joke, and I remember being so grateful for my breastfeeding breaks with Oscar, or the times Oscar needed to get out of the room, as I found it utterly impossible to be in there. The man behind this way of healing we were learning about seemed so insincere, to me, and sat on stage inviting people up to tell their horrible stories of trauma, pain and grief, and ask him for help, for support, for guidance, for him to simply tell them 'just let it go'. It was basically all I remember him saying for the entire three days, and it felt so wrong that these people had paid him good money to feel better.

There is merit to letting go – there definitely is – but in my opinion, watching those people on stage be bamboozled by what this man was saying made me realise the validation part of someone listening to you is just as important. These people wanted to be heard, and so did I. So badly.

It was during these days I also felt crystal clear on my lack of passion and purpose, because all these people in this room felt it too. And this man's response to 'let it go, and you will find it' felt so unattainable. I felt like I was more broken than before after this retreat.

I'd been trying so hard to let go of these feelings. And I felt like they were there to stay forever, which meant I'd never find my passion or my purpose as I was incapable of 'letting go'. What I learned in years to come is that letting go is the final step. It's the goal. It's not the start. You cannot start by letting go. The first step is to let in. Let in those you can share with, who can support you and validate you. Letting in is the key, rather than letting go.

And letting in was not something I was in the business of doing at that time. Not at all.

~

I was deeply relieved to leave Sedona behind, and return to our normal life, hopping from one city to the next. And I craved this because it meant no time to reflect on life, on myself.

We went from the US, to London, to Hong Kong, and then to Bali, all within ten days.

The retreat was already a distant memory, never to be spoken of again between Craig and me.

We returned home to Monaco in the middle of January and took a month or two off from the travel. It felt like a real slowdown for us, both in the sense of our personal lives and also with Triangl. The brand was not building the same way it had done the previous year. It felt like the growth phase was over, which was a relief, in a way, as the scaling to match that growth had felt impossible.

What we were now faced with was finding ways to capture new customers and retain them. Far more standard issues for a business, and ones more in my area of expertise of marketing and customer care. But it was this year in which my drive for anything business related fell even further through the floor, and I acted far more like an employee than a co-founder and director.

Every idea I'd had in previous years either never made it past the initial ideation phase, due to the lack of anyone being able to implement anything for or even with us, or caused such conflict between Craig and me that nothing ever evolved. This repeated scenario created a blockage for me, in which I just couldn't find motivation anymore to come up with marketing strategies and activations.

I now waited to be told what to do by Craig, most likely an act running parallel with my feeling of personal disempowerment, as it felt safer, easier and less inflammatory. I avoided voicing my opinion, suggesting solutions, and really almost any active involvement, and sought to manage only the more basic administrative tasks daily, and not add anything else to the business.

~

It was mid-March, and I'd finally weaned Oscar from breastfeeding, just shy of two years.

He was more than ready, and by this stage was only feeding once a day, at night before bed.

I remember that last night so clearly, when he instinctively rolled over to feed himself to sleep. I firmly but kindly said 'no more'. He quietly cried for only a few minutes, before rolling back over and falling asleep. Craig was next to us, already fast asleep, and so I lay there alone, crying over the enormity of this moment. It wasn't only the end of our feeding journey, but the end of some form of dependence between us. Oscar made me feel useful, made me feel somewhat of a good person, and to lose even a fraction of that feeling was a big loss. Like most nights, I was awake until well after midnight, despite sleep deprivation being a huge factor in my day, as Oscar didn't sleep through the night until he was well over two years old. I'd stay up experiencing every emotion I'd pushed down during the day. It was easy enough to suppress it during the day and distract myself, but at night, those feelings were always right there. Keeping me awake, reminding me I was not happy, far from it.

But, as always, I'd eventually succumb to sleep, and the next day, I'd say to myself, was a fresh start, even though I knew it really wasn't.

Without needing to have Oscar with me 24/7, I jumped at the opportunity to attend a girlfriend's wedding in Thailand, and planned a week-long solo trip. To have that kind of freedom felt foreign to me; it was exciting but scary. I'd jumped in the deep end of being without Oscar. Here we were going from not a night apart to suddenly a bunch of them.

I almost didn't go. I felt scared to go and see friends, and act as though life was a dream, and I felt scared to leave my bubble. I'd built my identity around certain ways of being that heavily relied on Craig and Oscar being around, and being without them felt like a level of unknown I wasn't sure I was equipped to handle.

Once I was on the plane, though, a lot of those fears subsided, and I leaned into the idea of a break, one that I really did feel I needed.

The first few days were relaxing and peaceful. However it was on the third day that we decided to go to a day club. After a few drinks, we sat down to lunch, and all ordered the calamari salad. A few bites in, and I asked the girls if theirs tasted as fishy as mine, as mine was almost inedible. Both of them shook their heads no, and in that moment it hit me like a ton of bricks. I usually liked to drink champagne on the plane; it was always an attempt to relish my 'success' and feel like I was living this blessed life. Flying first class, drinking champagne – a typical ego moment and one I tried to cultivate. But this flight to Thailand saw me not even finish one glass; I just didn't feel like it. I ignored it in the moment, but now to also not be able to eat mild seafood on account of it being too fishy meant I couldn't ignore two very big signs of what was happening. It seemed impossible to even consider. I'd only just stopped breastfeeding Oscar; I was only just getting a taste of time alone. Surely I couldn't be pregnant. We went on with our day, and on the way back to the hotel, I stopped by a pharmacy for some tests. I wanted to wait until that night, after dinner. I didn't want to know yet. I knew, but I just needed to pretend for a few more hours that I didn't need to face this situation yet.

Of course, in the villa after dinner, after three tests, it was very clear I was pregnant with my second baby. I sat with the news silently for a while, trying to process it all.

I loved being pregnant, and I loved being a mum. I felt excited at the thought of another experience. I knew Craig wanted a big family, and I knew he'd be thrilled. And I knew being pregnant meant I was able to escape a lot of the work I didn't want to do anymore, not just within the business, but in all aspects of everyday life. Pregnancy was an exit clause to having to really participate in much at all. And this was the feeling deep down I hated having. Because I knew I didn't want to not participate in life. I knew I wanted more for my life than this – to be using a baby as an excuse to avoid my own life. Having another baby meant abandoning my sense of self for another two or even three years, and the thought of that was devastating.

But I had no other option. In those short hours since I realised what was happening, I knew this was the way it was, and I couldn't change things, and I just had to try my best.

I called Craig and he was thrilled, of course. I then spent the rest of the trip in a haze, processing how the year ahead would now go.

~

I returned home to Monaco and settled in for a few months. We had found a new apartment to move into, and Craig was in full design mode with it. The overwhelming majority of apartments in Monaco were fairly unattractive. Old, tall apartment buildings with basic amenities, and no character. We'd found a villa, in the heart of Monte Carlo literally above our local café, and far closer to everything we wanted to access in Monaco, so it made perfect sense to move.

Craig was also working very hard on renovating our boat for our summer trip.

His work ethic never even took a pause, and he always loved to have numerous projects on the go. I was the mildly enthusiastic partner, never wanting to take any interest, but showing just enough so as not to cause an argument between us.

I remember the first time we went to visit the boat yard after the boat had been wrapped in a matte-black wrap, an aesthetic decision Craig made that had rarely been done before in the boating scene, especially not in Monaco. He was so excited to show me, and I remember him being so angry at my less-than-enthusiastic reaction, and me feeling so disappointed in myself. Looking back, I know I would have been a terrible person to spend time with, often running on auto-pilot and missing moments that should have felt so exciting, so special, so fun.

Craig and I had started to have more honest conversations during this time about how we were so different to our old selves, how we were growing apart, how we were not often aligned, but in the same sense how we had gone through something no one else knew about, how we had a growing family to enjoy, how we still had so much joy in our lives. These discussions where we could still find common ground gave me some hope for a relatively happy future, and they were enough to keep me moving forward.

Being pregnant also allowed me to relax with my feelings more easily, and it gave me some purpose again that I'd been missing. It also put a dent in my disordered eating and freed up my mind and body to be able to enjoy food more, which always gifted me with much more clarity and energy in my day.

We took the boat out again for the summer. We had friends join us on a few occasions, visiting from Australia, and I felt happier than I had in a long time. The boat trips were always so enjoyable and gave me some of the happiest memories during my Triangl times while living in Monaco.

We had a full-time staff of five on board, so every need was taken care of. A captain, a second captain, a chef, and two deck hands ready to wait on us 24/7. From the moment we woke up, to the moment we went to sleep, it was complete luxury. We swam almost every day, and had some of our best friends with us. We were not drinking, and with our small child and another on the way, time on the boat was a very wholesome family experience. I have too many favourite days to count, but my favourite place to visit was always Capri. Our yacht looked like a tinny compared to the real superyachts, and it was a daily occurrence to witness a new giant yacht cruise into the area, and google it to see who the owner was. The biggest yacht we ever saw belonged to the co-founder of DreamWorks. Guests on board at the time were Oprah Winfrey and Tom Hanks; however, we never saw them make an appearance on deck. A personal highlight was also when P. Diddy posted a photo of our little matte-black yacht in 2017 to his Instagram, causing absolute giddiness in all of us on board.

I never thought I was a water baby until we had the boat. I paddle-boarded every single day if the weather allowed for it, and those moments when it was just myself and the ocean, especially at sunset, were some of the most beautiful times in my whole life. I will never forget them.

~

After the peak of summer, we returned to Monaco, I already was under the care of a German obstetrician, based in Monaco, who I'd seen twice before the summer. I was around five months pregnant by the time we saw her again. She was firm but nice enough; however, the hospital in Monaco was surprisingly rundown. It felt cold and dismal. The maternity-ward tour lacked any kind of warmth or care, and I'd spoken to a friend who had paid for a private room before the birth of her child but due to a lack of space had spent twelve hours of her labour in a hallway. Suffice to say, I had absolutely zero interest in having my baby boy there.

We'd found out the sex of the baby in Monaco, just as we did with Oscar, as soon as we could. One of the defining moments of me not wanting to have my baby in that hospital was when we found out the sex of the baby. I remember the distinction between both experiences so well. In Hong Kong it was a big moment, the hoopla you'd expect: 'Are you ready to find out?'

and all that jazz, whereas in Monaco, the sonographer just blurted out 'It's a boy' before we even got a chance to prepare for the moment.

I had never been one for sentimental moments, and finding out the sex of our babies beforehand was merely because neither Craig nor I were interested at all in surprises. In fact, we had both decided on the names early on in the pregnancies for both boys, and shared them with friends and family when anyone asked. It did feel nice to be able to bond with both babies while they were in my tummy; I liked being able to call them by name, and talk to them, knowing just that little bit about them.

Perhaps my pregnancy and birth experience with Oscar helped us make our decision to return to Hong Kong for three months. It worked not only for the end of my pregnancy and impending birth, but because we needed to spend time on Triangl again, after not giving it much love or attention for months.

We stayed in Hong Kong in the serviced apartments we'd first moved into when Triangl started doing well, and it felt like home. We'd already checked with my Hong Kong OB prior to leaving Monaco to ensure he was able to take me on as a patient, and I slotted into my regular check-ups as if I'd almost never left.

While being back in Hong Kong felt safe, again my discomfort with my life, and especially how it would be after this baby, felt more and more suffocating. I didn't want to keep travelling the way we had after having Oscar. It was going to be different with two. More work, more required by me.

I wanted a home base. I wanted to slow down. It was in contrast to what Craig wanted in life; he wanted to be a citizen of the world. To move around all the time. He felt it was possible to go everywhere with our children. I, on the other hand, did not feel the same. I wasn't able to do it all, in one place, let alone travelling at the rate we had been for the past three years. I didn't want to raise the boys and have Triangl on top of that, and I also didn't want to raise the boys and have no part in Triangl. Both options felt awful to me.

The distance between Craig and me grew every day, and the smallest comment or act by Craig would set me off into a spiral. I'd given up on him and me, and I just wanted out. However, I had no idea how to voice my feelings to him. I was terrified to be the one responsible for wanting to end our relationship, and knew it was far more than a relationship breakup, as we had our Triangl business relationship, as well as a toddler and a baby coming, who would both be affected greatly. So I didn't say anything.

But it didn't take Craig long to make the decision for us. I was eight months pregnant, and Craig was on the way to New York for work. His last trip before coming back for the birth. Oscar and I walked him down to the car to say goodbye. I don't even remember what Craig said or did; I am sure it would have been so minor that it wouldn't have even been worth mentioning if I could recall it, but it set me off. Every moment between us had become like this. Every time he said a word, made a face, looked at me a certain way, I was flooded with the hundreds of times he'd done that before. I had convinced myself how much of an awful person he was, and he was the enemy. I was so hypersensitive, so reactive to all he ever did and said, and he'd also had enough of being made out to be the enemy. Regardless of who was in the wrong, and who was the one causing the other to feel a certain way, those moments were awful for everyone. I'd burst into tears, wherever we were – usually in public – and Oscar would cuddle into me, his mum, in clear pain.

In that final blow-up, I know Craig did what he knew he had to do:

end our relationship to save our son from the pain of growing up with this trauma in his life.

He called me from the car, on the way to the airport, and told me he couldn't continue things as they were, and we needed to end our relationship.

Rather than feeling shocked, I was relieved. I finally felt like I was closer to being free, from whatever hell I'd put myself in. I'd convinced myself it was Craig who was the reason I suffered so greatly, and this felt like a big step forward into reclaiming myself.

The truth is that I had let our romantic relationship take a backseat from the time Triangl launched. I was never able to voice my needs to Craig, for fear of being rejected, but then resented him for not meeting my needs. It was really that simple and why I never fully participated in our relationship over decisions like getting married, or buying new properties, or anything else relating to our personal lives.

I didn't like being entwined in each other's lives, the way we were, 24/7, but he did.

So, that mismatch alone was enough to cause huge issues between us from very early on.

We were the couple that brought out the best in each other and the worst in each other, at different times.

We had opposing views a lot of the time, and, in my opinion, this was a big driver in Triangl's success, because we always saw things from a very different point of view, and had to fight for what we wanted in the business. On a personal level, it became increasingly hard for me to manage always having different – sometimes fundamentally different – views on everything.

It wasn't always doom and gloom, and there were things we always both enjoyed. We were both sun lovers who always sought Vitamin D where possible. We both always wanted the same type of food when we travelled, and always wanted to eat the same thing, and, of course, we both had a great love for fashion and business, and loved cruising the streets of wherever we were, checking out different brands for inspiration.

We worked hard to navigate that last month before I gave birth in an amicable way.

We'd never set up anything formally, in the event of a separation, so we were having to wing it, and work it out on our own.

The plan we both agreed on was that once I'd had the baby, we'd work out the steps of a formal separation. Craig moved into an apartment on another floor, and we waited to have our second child.

As Oscar was so early, we were mindful of the same this time around. My OB also warned me I was progressing in the same way as I was with Oscar, so from six weeks before my due date, I was told to stay almost sedentary, and relax as much as possible.

The mental battle of feeling like you could go into labour at any moment was rather challenging, and I convinced myself every single night that contractions were starting, and yet they never did. After a very boring six weeks, and a day past my due date, I arranged for an induction. I was well and truly over waiting, and this baby needed to get out, so my new life, whatever it was, could start.

We arrived at the hospital, Craig, Oscar and me – and the induction process began. I was admitted in the evening, at around 7pm. And the plan was to have the induction tablet then, and then the drip the next morning, to have the baby the following day.

The tablet was inserted at around 9pm, and I was wheeled into the room at around 10.30pm, to spend the night. An hour later, or perhaps even less, I started to feel contractions. Those familiar surges in pain, coming and going. They were more gentle this time, but still very much growing with each movement.

I buzzed for the nurse, who promptly called my OB, who came in, and, after a quick exam, arranged for me to be wheeled back into the delivery suite as I was in labour.

I immediately requested the epidural, a bit of a necessity, considering I had Oscar next to me, still very much awake and extremely interested in his surroundings.

Once the medication had taken force, and the calm had taken over, I settled into the night. Craig took Oscar to a room for some sleep, and to get some himself. I didn't ask him to stay, and he didn't offer.

I was again alone, as I'd been for Oscar's birth, and it felt okay. I knew I was able to do this again, and I felt the strength in being alone, whether it was something I had forced upon myself or not.

I felt empowered in both those labour experiences; being alone felt like it was how it was supposed to be. It felt like a reminder that I was strong, that I was able to do things that were hard, and do them because I was capable.

It had only been a few hours when I started to feel pressure right below my coccyx bone. I hadn't felt this with Oscar, but it hit me hard this time around. I didn't even know this meant the baby was coming. So I tried to ignore it for a good few minutes before I realised this sensation wasn't going away and I buzzed for the midwife.

In came the OB, who again had chosen to stay the night, to be there for me – a decision again I was completely floored by and ultimately just so grateful for.

It was happening, and I was minutes away from giving birth. The doctor leaned in. 'Do you want me to wake Craig? Do you want him here for the birth?'

Craig and I hadn't discussed how this part of the birth would work now that we were separated, which in hindsight wasn't very smart of us. Perhaps we were both avoiding it to not have to say what we wanted. I knew I didn't want him there; I wanted to go it alone, for the second time. So I asked for them to leave him, and wake him as soon as the baby was born.

It didn't take long to push this baby out, and while I felt nothing with Oscar, I felt pressure in my body like nothing else, and it felt far tougher than the first time. I was more aware this time, and when they placed Oly onto my chest I knew to look for any signs of illness and any movements by others in the room that would alert me to something being wrong.

But nothing was wrong; he was perfect. He was a perfect size, a perfect baby. Immediately his presence calmed me and I felt euphorically good.

Craig had been called in during these first minutes, and came in with a broad smile on his face. He hadn't missed really much at all; Oly was only minutes old, and I knew I'd made the right decision to leave him sleeping while I gave birth to our little boy.

I was wheeled into the ward room, an hour or so after, and Oly was taken to the nursery so I could get a few hours' rest. It was at this time Oscar woke up and walked over to my bed, climbing in and sleeping with me for an hour or so. The absolute joy in being able to be there for my first-born son in that moment, knowing I'd successfully given birth to a healthy baby, his brother, felt so raw, so beautiful, and it filled me with such love for my little family.

Later, Craig and Oscar went back to the apartment to freshen up while Oly and I were moved into a new room. My experience after having Oscar had felt frantic and chaotic, and Oscar had cried all the time, which I thought was just how all new babies were, so I sat and waited for Oly to do the same.

But Oly was calm; he was still. He only wriggled when he needed feeding, and then after feeding, and a gentle burp, I would lay him back down and he would drift off to sleep. I was absolutely awestruck by him, and filled with immense gratitude for a baby so calm and so peaceful.

That one night in hospital was blissful. I kept waiting for cries but he never gave me any. Oly gave me hope that I could make it as a single mum, and so after that first night we checked out of hospital, and went home.

Being in a serviced apartment was an easy place to transition to from hospital. It was cleaned daily, room service was available, and there was a team of people around to help if any trouble arose. After arriving home, on that same day Craig and Oscar left for New York for two weeks. A decision Craig made so I could have a reprieve from Oscar, who was the sweetest child, but still a needy two-and-a-half year old. I was in part appreciative of this, but largely I felt sad.

As much as I was able to do this alone, I didn't really want to. I wanted Oly to be enjoyed, shared, loved, by not just me but by his brother and his dad. But I didn't say anything, and let them leave.

It was a very peaceful time with Oly, albeit lonely. I distinctly remember feeding him in those long nights, when the rest of the world was seemingly asleep, except for us. I'd open the blinds to look out on to the lights of Hong Kong. We faced Victoria Harbour as well as the cityscape, and it was the perfect bright light to fill the room at nighttime.

I never allowed myself to feel anything other than gratitude for him. And it was the truth, anyway. I was so grateful to Oly, for allowing me to love like this, for teaching me what it could feel like every day, not just when thinking of him.

It was in those first few weeks with him that I felt like I wasn't completely gone, even though I still had no idea how to get back to myself – how to come back to me.

Chapter Twelve

New Beginnings

My life felt like it was holding some promise, for the first time in so long.

Before having Oly, and after our separation, Craig and I had loosely discussed the possibility of me taking over Triangl.

Craig had lots of other interests, whether it be re-designing our yacht, investing our finances into suitable opportunities, or whatever else he happened to be into at the time (he was very much a true entrepreneur, always questioning why things were done a certain way and seeking how to do them better) and was busy with projects, but I didn't have anything at all, not even a hobby. It made a fair amount of sense for me to take over the business, and I even surprised myself at my desire to take it on.

We continued discussing it, and as soon as Craig returned to Hong Kong, we sat down properly and went over the plans of how to transition me into the role, and transition Craig out. Nothing was formally arranged, and we were not discussing practicalities of percentage splits, and buy-outs etc, but merely how I would step into running the business day to day, and Craig would not. We had our CFO, John, with us, and also were joined by another adviser, an English native and Hong Kong resident, who Craig had found years before when we were looking for tax advice. They had been there to support Craig until this point, but were now going to support and guide me through this new phase, of taking over Triangl and assisting me in navigating all I had to learn and take on.

We were at the Four Seasons in Hong Kong, in the dining room, and I had Oly next to me, only just over two weeks old. I remember insisting I was able to take on the business, despite having a newborn, and feeling really like I was capable enough. I didn't feel it was anything I couldn't do, and while perhaps that was true, I was deep in my post-partum period, and the adrenaline, and can-do attitude, was not ever-lasting and was only really biologically there to support the needs of my new baby, not a multi-million-dollar business I was taking over.

Craig and I had always entertained the idea of moving Triangl to the US and setting up our office there. The US was by far still our biggest market, and we always felt we could do more if we were on the ground, maximising the potential right in front of us.

I had no desire to return to Monaco, or back to Australia, and I felt like it was smart to move to the States, so I decided to move to New York and have it as my base, splitting my time between Monaco and New York, initially. I didn't want to ever return to Monaco, in reality, but as I was taking the boys with me, Craig and I had to compromise.

But before any move, it was time to go back to Australia. We'd been away for two years now, and I wanted to take Oly home to meet my family. Hong Kong to Australia was only a nine-hour flight, and only a two-hour time-zone change, so it was an easy trip to make.

I flew back solo with a three-week-old Oly, and a two-year-old Oscar, checking into a hotel in Melbourne for a few nights, before going to Sydney for Christmas. Craig stayed in our apartment at one end of Bondi Beach so he could spend time with the boys and I rented another apartment at the other end of the beach.

We spent a few weeks in Bondi, but with a newborn unable to spend much time in the sun and the heat, I spent most of our stay inside.

Craig and I had planned to go our separate ways towards the end of January. Oly and I were to go straight to New York so I could start setting up our US office, and Craig planned to bring Oscar to me a few weeks later.

I was excited to leave Australia and start this new chapter of my life. I arrived with Oly in New York in the dead of winter. It was absolutely freezing! I found an apartment on West Broadway, which, aside from being up a flight of stairs and so not ideal for a stroller and a baby, was perfect.

Shortly after arriving, I started to look for both a nanny and an assistant. I knew that the benefit of cities as large as New York was there was never any shortage of good people looking for work and I quickly found my new assistant, Pamela, a young Australian girl living in New York with her older sister.

I would not have been able to survive New York without Pamela. I had no friends, no support network, no one. Although this was something I was used to, New York was all about the hustle and I just knew I needed a right-hand girl, which Pamela absolutely was.

Every morning, she'd be at my apartment bright and early, coffee in hand, ready to take on the day, with her never-failing positive way of thinking and living. She was the ultimate hype girl, and I was so grateful to have her next to me during those months.

Combined with a nanny I had found through an agency to care for the boys, we hit the ground running, arranging meetings with lawyers and tax agents – getting all the documentation needed to be able to set up a base in the city. We also arranged castings to be able to see in real life all the models we'd ever looked at online, so we could build a database to rely on for all future shoots that year.

We met with PR firms and with marketing firms, all with the plan to start to take Triangl into a new era. I had so many big visions, big dreams. I was energised, and if there was ever a city to make a girl feel anything was possible, it was New York.

Oscar soon joined us and our little family of three was based in New York for the next few months, feeling out how we were going to make life work there. It was in March, however, after much back and forth with many different parties, that I was told if I based myself full-time in New York, that all the profits from Triangl would fall under the tax jurisdiction in the US, which meant the rate of tax I'd be subject to would be a lot more than Monaco's and Jersey's zero per cent tax. I was advised to leave the US, and return to Monaco, while the rest was sorted out. Under tax laws, I wasn't able to spend more than 120 days a year in the US, or I'd be considered a tax resident. Of course, I was able to stay if I'd really wanted to, but it was going to impact the operations of the business if I chose this, most significantly in terms of adding pressure to where money was spent. Because we'd fought so hard to set up Triangl in tax-positive jurisdictions, it felt irresponsible to then blow that all on living in a city purely because I wanted to so I could perhaps enjoy a better lifestyle.

This was extremely deflating to me. I didn't want to leave. I loved New York and wanted to stay. I especially didn't want to return to Monaco. I had nothing there, other than a bunch of mainly sad memories of a deteriorating relationship and my unhappiness with myself.

I had a few weeks to prepare, which was difficult considering I was returning to Monaco without a home. Pamela and I found an apartment for me to rent, in a very old building but it had beautiful views across Port Hercules, and I felt comforted knowing I'd be able to look out at the city in such a lovely way.

Going back to Monaco felt like a backwards step. It wasn't what I wanted to do at all, but I was determined to make it work, and promised myself we'd be back in New York by summer. I was still committed to Triangl, but it was becoming more and more apparent that returning to Monaco had created a negative shift in me, and my desire to run the business started to wane.

Meetings with our CFO now involved Craig as well, as his interest in the business picked up again once we were back in the same city as each other.

All the freedom I'd felt in New York, the sense of hope for a brighter and bigger future for Triangl and myself, had all but disappeared, and I saw myself falling back into my old life, one where I was involved with Triangl, but not really, and I could not go back there again.

Craig and I had planned to start mediation and work through the splitting of our assets – something we hadn't yet done, and needed to do – so we decided to set this meeting in London, on somewhat neutral ground.

And so it was that we brought along our CFO and adviser to a dark, downstairs room in Soho that looked a lot more like a nightclub than a set of meeting rooms to discuss the serious business of dividing everything we owned between us so we could move forward with our lives.

We had no set objectives, other than to get some kind of agreement down on paper.

I sat there, keeping quiet, not sure what I wanted, what was fair, what I wanted to say.

I couldn't find the words; I didn't even know. I'd gone from building Triangl, to resenting it, to ignoring it, to wanting to take it to the moon again, to now feeling like I didn't even know what to think. All I knew was I had to find a way to move forward, and not go backwards.

'I want out.' As soon as I said it once, I knew it was the only way.

And I did want out. I wanted out of it all. I wanted to get out of that dark room, I wanted to get out of my business, I wanted to get out of being with Craig, I wanted to get out of my broken mind.

We wrote down an agreement on a piece of paper, with a pencil, splitting our assets as best we knew how. I only wanted cash. It's all I wanted. So I could start again. I wanted to feel free.

I left that meeting room as quickly as I could. I basically ran out of there. I wanted to go and enjoy this freedom that I'd finally asked for. That I'd finally acknowledged out loud. I was out!

It was a beautifully sunny spring day in London, and I walked the streets back to my hotel, trying to soak this feeling in. It had been so long since I'd felt free, and I wanted to really enjoy it. I sat down outside my hotel, at the bar, and ordered a glass of champagne.

I texted my sister, back in Melbourne, and told her I had left the business. She asked me how I felt, and I wrote back, 'Good, I think? I'm in shock.'

I took a sip of champagne, and tried to soak it all in. I honestly expected it to hit me like a wave of joy. I was finally free of my toxic relationships with my partner and my business, and surely this had to be what was going to fix me.

I wasn't ready to face the fact that perhaps it was not Craig or Triangl that was the reason I was struggling, that perhaps it was actually me. That I was the problem in my own life. That my years of suppressing my mental ill health, my true feelings and addressing the issues I had were perhaps the real reason I didn't feel free.

So I sipped the champagne in that glass and waited for the feeling of freedom.

It never came.

Chapter Thirteen

Playing Pretend

I spent the next months busying myself with domestic duties, furnishing my apartment in Monaco and figuring out my next move. I'd agreed to stay in Monaco so that Craig could be near the boys, and didn't feel comfortable or perhaps strong enough to make a decision to separate the family like that. Oly was a very easy baby. In contrast to Oscar, he slept like a dream and caused little to no fuss. Oscar was also well travelled and well adjusted to the life he'd always known, which was being on the move quite often.

My next move. I took a lot of time to try and figure out what this was. On paper, my situation was prosperous. Money, youth, experience. I really was able to do what I wanted. I told myself I wanted to take time and just de-stress after all that had happened. But still my mind felt so chaotic, so busy, so full, even while everything around me slowed down.

My days in Monaco had been freed up, with nannies to care for the boys during working hours. A stark contrast to my first year with Oscar, where I was doing it all, this was absolutely the opposite scenario. I wasn't working, I wasn't really doing anything.

I'd plan my days meticulously with nothing much to do. At 9.30am I'd walk to get coffee. At 10.30 I'd visit some type of luxury store. At midday

I'd go to the yacht club or beach club to lie in the sun for a few hours. I'd then return home to wait for the arrival of my children and start the dinner/bath/bed routine.

These days were long, they were lonely and they were the most unfulfilling days I'd ever had. I relied on my regular acquaintances in the luxury stores, the café and the restaurants for my daily conversations and interactions. I lingered in all of these places, trying to fill my cup with some connection to carry me through the day. Of course, they were always nothing but lovely to me; I'm sure I often helped them reach their budgets. I bought something almost every day, whether it be from Celine, Prada, Balenciaga or Miu Miu. I was, of course, on a first-name basis with all the sales assistants, and there were a few who I had come to know very well. And so I'd linger in those particular stores, always mindful to purchase enough so they stayed with me and kept me company. They were all I had in the way of adult friendships, and I worked hard to keep them intact, as did my wallet.

I tried so hard to find joy in these days. I did all the things I knew gave me my usual dopamine hits. I bought all the nice things I possibly could, I drank during the day, not excessively but just a few glasses to feel a 'buzz'. I built a perfect, natural tan. I restricted my eating, but not to the point of illness, just to keep me looking as lean as possible. I continued these same patterns, to try and find just a little bit of joy, some enjoyment, but it just seemed to be moving further out of my reach.

The reality was that these actions started to bring me anxiety like I'd never felt before.

I'd receive packages I'd bought online and I wouldn't even want to open them. They'd build and build, and when I'd finally open them, I'd unwrap a pair of $2000 boots, or a $3000 jacket, and not even take into account what I was opening. I was becoming numb to things that usually brought me some type of positive feeling.

This extended to alcohol, where I would pour a glass of wine for myself after the children were asleep, and sit on the couch and not even drink it. The interest wasn't there, to indulge in anything that I used to look forward to.

Those nights were tough. An unfulfilled day behind me, and an unfulfilled day to follow. I tried so hard to have gratitude for where I was, for how fortunate I was. I'd sit on my balcony, looking out at the harbour in Monaco, arguably one of the greatest views in the world, watching the sky turn a beautiful golden orange and then pink, and I'd feel nothing but sadness. I felt so trapped in my own life, and I just didn't know how to get out. I'd go to bed, and lie next to Oscar, who always slept in my bed, and I'd feel thankful for him every night, for if I didn't have him and his brother, sleeping peacefully in the other room, I would have found ways to completely self-destruct. I was alive for them, and them only.

I first attached these feelings to my hatred of Monaco, and so I started looking into moving to London. I remember going there for a weekend with Oscar, leaving Oly behind with the nanny, and walking the streets of Notting Hill, feeling like maybe this could be home.

Returning to Australia was still a no-go, not only because it took the boys far away from their dad, but because I couldn't go home feeling like this. I needed to go home triumphant, successful, happy. Australia was a backwards step for me, in every way, and not even an idea I entertained when trying to escape Monaco.

The reality was it was too easy to stay in Monaco. I was well and truly exhausted. I didn't want to move again; I didn't want to take control of my life and make changes because I was just so tired. I was burnt out, in every sense of the word, and knowing it would take a lot of effort to move, I just couldn't face it.

Craig and I were still in a very co-dependent relationship in a way too. While we lived in separate homes, we spent almost every day together in some way. It was too easy to do so. The boys loved all being together, and I felt that at least this was something I could be proud of doing, parking my own needs for those of my children.

Earlier in the year, in New York, during times of hope and some purpose, I'd become interested in doing some healing work. It turned out that Craig's years of encouraging me to look into spirituality rubbed off, and, with my newfound lust for life during those first few months of the year, I'd decided to look further into healing.

I had found a healer online, and was immediately drawn to her. I immediately booked a session with her, which didn't come cheaply, but I felt that this higher price tag equalled a more transformative session.

I had Pamela, my assistant, arrange the bookings and I was so nervous on the day of the session, I had her come with me, just to be sure it was all legitimate.

I found this session with the healer profoundly accurate. She knew things about me, about my family, about my life – and the session ran for eight hours. By far the longest spiritual session I've ever had to date, and quite the introduction into the world of spirituality.

She opened my eyes to something I'd never known to exist, through her knowing not only intimate details of my family and life, but also knowing how my mind was operating, and knowing the chaos I was internally going through, and keeping to myself. I felt my life was going to change course as a result of this.

Driving back to my apartment that night, it was pouring with rain. A torrential downpour, and it was the most terrified I'd ever felt in my life. I had never ever truly entertained spirituality, or spirit – and suddenly it was right in front of me, this other side of life, and I didn't want it to be. But something had been cracked open in me that night. I sat at home for hours afterwards, with a ringing in my ears that I could not explain, and I just knew I'd opened myself up to the spiritual world, in some way.

I'd left behind this healing work when I moved back to Monaco, and avoided doing any more. But this healer and I stayed in touch. We spoke often, eventually daily. I trusted her implicitly, and relied on her guidance. My self-worth, self-belief, didn't exist, and so I relied on her to see it in me through her observations of who she saw me to be, a mindful, intelligent, energetic person. A person I knew I used to be, and who I so dearly wanted to be again.

After a couple of months, she came and visited me in Monaco, and we spent days together, discussing the future. I began to consider her a true confidante, a mentor, a friend. She was my way out of how I was feeling; she was my beacon of light to a better life, because she saw me in a way I wanted to see myself as again, as a person of substance, a person who was special, who had something great to offer the world.

The lines between our professional relationship and friendship (as it was in my eyes) became blurred, and ultimately our connection fizzled out altogether. She had grand plans for us to go into business together, and was pushing for the involvement to become official, most definitely before I was ready. Whether it was her taking advantage of me, or her more hopeful intentions of bringing my skills and ambition back – I invested a considerable sum of money, US$50,000 into the ideation of a business, which I never saw again. She was far more advanced in her ways of thinking and operating, whether for good or for bad, and I was still a very confused, very fragile person.

It may be easier for me to blame her for taking advantage of me during a time I was extremely vulnerable but I am ultimately grateful to her. She saw in me what I was to eventually learn in myself, in time: that I was worthy, I was special, I was going to be okay, and, in fact, better than ever. I couldn't receive that learning at the time, but she allowed me to easily move into that space later in life and I will always have gratitude for all that she gave me in paving the way.

The reality was, however, that I was still stuck in Monaco. My patterns of thinking and behaving kept me there. Everything felt hard. It was easier to stay. I genuinely felt like I could just convince myself that this was happiness. That I was living a beautiful life, that I was feeling good. I had mental strength in me somewhere, I knew. I'd always been a headstrong person, a passionate person, a person with strong convictions, and I believed on some level I could apply this strong will to force myself to feel peace with my life.

~

It was mid-August, and summer was almost over. Craig and I became more and more intertwined in each other's lives. Dinners out as a family, beach days together. So much time together. We wondered if we should try to reconcile.

I hadn't dated at all since our split. As someone who had always been in a relationship, or actively seeking one (a true Libran – a lover of love), to not be seeking any form of connection with a male companion was something I had never experienced, and I felt despair at times that I had lost my will for romantic love.

I knew in my heart and in my soul that my time with Craig was well and truly over.

Our relationship had run its course. But what other option did I have when the idea of a reconciliation was brought up? What else was going on in my life? I felt I owed it to Oscar and Oly to try.

And so we all travelled together, as a family, to Hong Kong. For it wasn't just an attempted personal reconciliation, but also one where perhaps I could come back on board with Triangl. I had done nothing since exiting five months prior, and had no business interests or involvement at all, so I felt I had no good reason to say no. And so off we went.

We stayed in the same serviced-apartment building this time as before we moved to Monaco back in 2015.

However, the apartment was at the back, with views to an imposing mountain, covered in dense greenery, rather than the busyness of the cityscape I had always loved and found comfort in looking out at. Somehow the tranquillity felt oppressive.

Craig and I had separate bedrooms, but otherwise were together most hours of the day.

We went straight to work. The Triangl office had moved a few years prior, out of Central, to a space in Kowloon, the mainland China side. This made more sense for all the staff, as they all lived on that side. But otherwise it was like nothing had changed. I spent the day trying on samples, fitting new styles. Craig had been testing out activewear, and as it always used to be, I was the fit model.

Those days were some of the darkest I can remember. It was the ultimate betrayal to myself, to be back there, but I felt it was what I deserved. I'd not done anything after finally separating from Craig and exiting Triangl. I'd not made any progress; I'd not tried at all to move forward. So, being back here was my punishment. For giving up on myself.

Craig had been seeing someone prior to us arriving back in Hong Kong. This hurt my ego and made me jealous, but mostly because I couldn't believe he'd moved on. He told me, on that second day in Hong Kong, that he was still speaking to her, still continuing with whatever it was that they had.

I was devastated. Not because of what he was doing – that was his choice and we weren't technically back together. But because of what I was doing, to myself.

How I was even here, with someone who didn't even really want to be with me either, sent shockwaves through my whole body.

It was from this point that my body kept the score. I'd ignored my mental health for years; I'd pushed the uncomfortable feelings away, and buried them deep down.

My sense of self was non-existent, as was my self-worth – and my body had, quite simply, had enough.

I started experiencing anxiety. I didn't know before this that anxiety could show up so physically. I felt like I didn't sleep for the entire time I was there. For two weeks. My eyes would close, and my heart would race. Pumping through my chest, filling me with such dread, I thought I was dying. On more than one occasion I went into Craig's room, to wake him to say, 'I'm scared, I think I'm dying,' to which he told me gently to go back to bed. While I'd been able to push away negative thoughts for years now, this wasn't something I was able to ignore.

I'd toss and turn, unable to escape the torture my mind was in, and now my body.

I was unable to eat during the day, with a loss of appetite I never knew existed. I had to force myself to eat scoops of ice-cream, mouthfuls of nuts. My mind was rejecting food; or was it my body? I couldn't even process it. All my senses were completely numb. I lost my smell, my taste, my touch. I was physically shutting down.

I lost five kilos in that time. I was already lean, and this put me into the scarily skinny category. And I was worried. This was a true health scare, and one I knew, categorically, I'd created within myself. I couldn't ignore this one, and it became very clear to me that I needed help. I needed support.

I was sitting on the floor in the apartment with Oscar and Oly, and Craig was on the couch. 'I have to go home, I have to go back to Melbourne,' I said.

I didn't know how long it would take. I didn't know what I'd do there. I just knew I had to go home. I booked flights that night for Oscar, Oly and me for the very next day and sent my mum a text.

'I'm coming home tomorrow.'

No more hiding, no more playing pretend; it was time to go home.

Chapter Fourteen

Homecoming

I was back in Melbourne, in September 2018, during the AFL finals season, a big time for Melbournians, and was sneaking in without telling anyone except my close family.

I'd booked a new hotel, in one of Melbourne's leafiest and loveliest areas. An area I wanted to be based in, and one I dreamed of living in pre-Triangl days. I didn't know quite what to do next, and as my patterns and programs were still very much rooted in avoidance, I did what I knew how to do best and pretended everything was fine. I had a reputation to uphold, after all – I was Miss Triangl, and my ego wanted to protect this identity, and sit with it, for as long as possible while I worked out what to do next.

I met someone on the second day home. Walking from my hotel to a bottle shop, and back again, I was stopped in my tracks by a man who knew who I was, who I didn't immediately know or recognise, but who was an old acquaintance from high-school years. We instantly became extremely close, spending every chance together we had, and talking to each other constantly, and our quasi-relationship set the tone for me to be as avoidant as possible to my life around me.

The next month was a blur. Avoidance of my issues took shape for me not in the way of closing off from life as I'd done in Monaco, but taking life in, head on, by partying.

I'd rented a beautiful home to stay in, which was the start of us moving around five times in as many months, from short-term furnished rental to short-term furnished rental.

My mum and sister practically moved in, to care for me, but mainly to care for my boys, as I spent most nights out, drinking excessively and taking drugs. I felt I was letting off steam, and I was, but in a destructive way.

I'd found new friends through this guy I was seeing, and there was safety in that because these people didn't know anything about me, other than that I was a multi-millionaire, successful business founder, returned to Australia for unknown reasons.

Aside from my mum and my sister, I kept everyone else who knew me at arm's length. To me, it didn't feel like overly destructive behaviour; it felt like a rite of passage.

I used to be social, I used to love going out, and I'd abandoned that side of me for so long, so I wanted to enjoy it, now I finally had it again. Another attempt by me to try to find freedom and healing in ways I wasn't going to find it.

~

A month in, and the guy I was seeing decided to basically drop me, overnight. The connection we had was strong, but also not very real. I knew it wasn't ever-lasting, so while there was shock to being ghosted, I knew it meant this chapter of my life was over. And it was time to slow down, even if just for a moment.

I so badly didn't want to commit to living back in Melbourne. I still very much wanted my identity to be Triangl, and I wanted to be the woman who lived in Monaco. I had, perhaps, expected to be feeling happier in Melbourne, but I wasn't. In fact, it was indeed worse, to be back home, where I essentially grew up. It felt like a huge backwards step, and I longed to at least be able to pretend I was happy in relative anonymity in Monaco, where I could falsify those happy feelings a little easier, through the life of luxury I'd built around me and with little to no social interaction every day. In Melbourne I was around people I knew, every day, and so the level of effort it took and was going to take to pretend to be a happy person was not going to be sustainable for very long, which put the fear of god in me.

I told everyone I was only home for the summer. And this was partly true, as it was what I'd told Craig I was doing, to avoid any discussions at the time over custody of our children.

I felt very much detached from my body during this period. I often found it hard to process what was happening around me, to connect the streams of thoughts in my head to anything tangible. It wasn't a heavy or dark feeling, but a feeling of flightiness. Lightheaded, and completely carefree. It was an unusual place to be in. I'd felt I'd moved somewhat forward by being back in Australia, in terms of taking care of my health, but I felt so displaced in this city I'd grown up in, and I didn't know where to fit in. I felt safer knowing my family were close and that this was my hometown, and that carried me through these first months home.

~

I first met Zac on a fairly hot November day. I was sitting outside a café/ bar in an inner suburb of Melbourne, with a friend, and saw him pull up in his car. I saw his face through the windscreen and felt an instant attraction, which wasn't a hard thing to do as he is probably one of the best-looking men I'd ever seen. I like to think I knew in that moment that I'd met my future husband, but to be totally honest, I was searching desperately for a love affair at the time. It was something I knew would be a good distraction for the summer and keep my mind and my heart busy.

We were introduced via my friend, who incidentally knew him, and he sat with us, alongside a few of his friends – and joined us for a few drinks. My initial attraction was thwarted by his demeanour, which appeared to be a little stand-offish and perhaps even a touch arrogant. Needless to say we didn't connect on that first meeting, and I left after only an hour to have dinner with my boys, who were under the care of a nanny most days at that time, not dissimilar to my behaviour earlier that year in Monaco. I put Zac out of my mind after that day, and didn't think of him again.

It wasn't until a month later that I bumped into him again, at a Christmas party. He came up to me with a warm greeting, offered to get me a drink and started chatting to me. Something about him had changed. He was a different person that night. He was sincere, he was kind, he was thoughtful, and he was genuine. Our first proper conversation wasn't anything even close to small talk, with Zac asking me questions no one had asked me yet, or perhaps it was the way in which he asked. I was in the throes of my healing/self-discovery journey at this time, via therapy and kinesiology. It was something that was bringing great awareness to my life, and I was navigating it and wanting to talk about it – all the time.

Zac was asking simple questions, probing as to why I had left my business, and how did I feel about my life now. We were in the middle of a noisy party, and it felt like everything had fallen away.

How did he care about these things when he hardly knew me? I felt seen. Until that moment, no one I'd met had any genuine, romantic interest in me as a person, and I really didn't have any interest in them either.

But this felt extremely different, at least for me. After that night, I was absolutely smitten. I pursued him relentlessly from that point on, knowing that I needed to at least date this man. Zac was the same age as me, a business owner of a car-wash company. Having grown up in Melbourne, in somewhat similar social circles, we'd never crossed paths even though perhaps we should have. He was undeniably and extremely handsome, but also incredibly kind and with integrity like I'd never seen in a man before.

Zac made me feel vulnerable in a good way, and I wanted to feel vulnerable. I wanted to finally be honest about myself and live in a way that felt more authentic to me.

It was a busy time of year, and we didn't get to meet again until Boxing Day. Craig had flown back to Australia so we could spend Christmas together as a family. The boys hadn't seen their dad for almost two months by this stage, so I obliged to having Christmas with him and them in Sydney, as opposed to insisting we stay in Melbourne. I flew the boys to Sydney on Christmas Eve, and, for the second year running, spent Christmas without family, in Sydney. I was very much accepting of this, as I wanted to keep things between Craig and me amicable. Discussions were starting to focus on what was going to happen after summer; was I going to return to Monaco as I'd insinuated when we left Hong Kong? I wanted to keep those decisions at bay for as long as possible, so a Sydney Christmas felt like a safe pay-off to buy me a few more weeks of peace.

I flew back to Melbourne on Boxing Day, heading out with friends and only meeting up with Zac in the depths of the night. When I pulled up to the bar, seeing him again set my heart alight. I never got butterflies with Zac; in fact, it was always the opposite – he calmed my nervous system immediately and he made me feel safe and grounded. He had an effect on me that I'd never felt before.

I stayed at his house that night, but only to sleep next to him. At most, we held hands.

Zac had suffered profound grief and tragedy in his life. Only one year prior, his older sister, Emily, had died following a long bout of mental-health struggles, resulting in alcoholism and leading to her death, and then his grieving mum, Kaye, had taken her own life, weeks later.

I'd been warned away from Zac by a few mutual friends, for he was reputed to be a party boy, and because of the grief he had in his heart, I was told it would probably be safer for me to steer clear of him, given I was in a vulnerable state as well.

We were both suffering when we met, highly protective of our hearts. It was when he told me of his tragedy, though, in his own words, that I had a new perspective on my own struggles, and I started to learn to frame my challenges differently.

What I was going through was self-inflicted, and therefore I had the power to self-fix it. Zac's trauma was far different, far less within his control. And it made mine feel, for the first time, something I had power over, something I could heal from.

I had such compassion for him, and it was a gift for myself in a way because it brought with it an awareness that my trauma was one that could be directly healed, with me in control.

What started as a powerful friendship, which Zac took the lead on, and which I very begrudgingly went along with given my feelings for him were far more than platonic, quickly grew into a powerful love affair.

Zac insisted his heart couldn't let me in, and I waited and waited to show him it could. And when it finally did, it was a love I'd never known before. It was unconditional, it was honest, it was all-consuming but it was never co-dependent.

I took my fair share of toxic behaviours into those first months, and Zac lovingly made it clear he wouldn't tolerate it. He allowed me the space to grow into the person I wanted to be again, or perhaps even just be for the first time.

He introduced me to exercise, consistent exercise, something he had placed great importance on during his management of his own mental health. He taught me how to find confidence through accomplishment, through making that time for myself every day, to start my day with that achievement under my belt.

We approached life so differently, but also in the same way, and we fell in love deeply and easily. I'd lie nestled into his back every night, grinning to the universe as a thank you for gifting me this man.

I initially felt he'd come into my life too soon, that I was still so broken and needed to heal on my own – but it ended up being him who encouraged me to heal, who accepted me always for who I was, who gave me space to fall down, and get back up again.

~

While Zac and I were falling in love, and starting our lives together – the impact of my life with Craig being over started to land.

I wanted to stay in Melbourne; I didn't want to leave. And I wanted to keep the boys with me. This, of course, was not the news Craig wanted to hear, as he wanted to stay in Monaco, and he was fully reliant on me returning with the boys at the end of the Australian summer. We were absolutely and completely stuck on any kind of custody agreement, as we both wanted the boys.

Every day, for weeks, we'd have conversations about the predicament, and they became more and more heated as time went on. Craig wanted us all to return and became fixated on this as the only solution. I wanted to stay in Melbourne, and while I would never demand to keep the boys with me, I made it clear that this was ultimately what I wanted.

The fear in me to even say those words out loud, but also the growth in knowing how important it was to say what I really wanted, felt both liberating and terrifying.

But I didn't want a nasty legal fight to keep my children in the way that was more commonly done when separated parents couldn't agree on custody arrangements. There wasn't a thought in my mind to call a lawyer and have a custody process followed.

I didn't want conflict; I didn't want to go back to Monaco. And so when Craig suggested he take the boys to live with him in Monaco, and have his extended time with them, like I'd just done, his five or so months, and then revisit the arrangement after that, I didn't have any other answer I could say than yes.

Craig and I had a distinct lack of boundaries, boundaries that I'd failed to ever set up.

I didn't feel I had a choice, other than to let my boys go with their father.

And part of me wanted a break – from everything attached to my former life.

From the daily fear of waking up to messages from Craig, not knowing how much of my day it would take up, having another conversation that I knew would have no resolution.

And so, at the start of February 2019, I went from being a mother of two to being childless – in the sense of not having my sons with me every day. I had flown the boys to Sydney, and then flew home alone to Melbourne, not allowing myself any space to be sad. I didn't want to feel the enormity of what was happening, and so I just told myself it was for four weeks, and I'd see them again then. It was how I got through the months, by breaking them down into those visits, where I would fly to Monaco every four weeks to spend a fortnight with them, and then return to Melbourne. The mathematical breakdown of time made it manageable, and it made it feel somewhat okay, even though it felt unfathomably deep within my heart.

It was the first time I had to have faith in myself and to own what was happening.

I had to bring awareness to my life and control only what I could, which was investing in my mental health, and in Zac, and in a life in Melbourne. It was the most challenging time of my life, though, without my children.

The guilt I wrestled with daily, questioning whether I should move back to Monaco, and what I was doing on the other side of the world without my sons, never stopped. I cried myself to sleep most nights, for the entirety of the time without them.

But I'd committed to the decision and I had to take accountability for that.

~

It was also during this time that my settlement with Craig over Triangl ran into problems.

We'd gone through a fairly amicable settlement process the year before, but with me moving back home, and our ongoing fights over the children, things had soured and so had our settlement agreement.

To save money during this period of unknowns, I moved into Zac's apartment, a tiny one-bedroom place. My Triangl settlement was in jeopardy, with discussions over monies owed to me ending in constant arguments, and never any resolution. My boxes and boxes of designer goods felt absolutely frivolous and completely ridiculous in this place. But there was nowhere else for it all to go, and it was all I had. My apartment in Monaco had been emptied a few months prior, and the entire contents were sitting in a storage container outside of Monte Carlo, waiting for my next move.

I felt quite frozen about what to do. The container held beautiful, expensive items from my former life, but the shipping was wildly expensive and it was money I felt nervous to spend in a time of such uncertainty. By this stage, the settlement situation was essentially frozen, and I had no clarity or certainty over when and if I'd ever see any more money paid to me. I had received some money after we first settled back in 2018, in London – however it was nowhere near anything close to what I was owed, which was a rather terrifying prospect after all I'd been through with Triangl.

I spent these initial months of 2019 avoiding my fairly substantial personal issues, with no children and no security over my finances. I instead dived head-first into my Melbourne life with Zac, which revolved heavily around big weekends of partying and weekdays spent waiting for the weekend. Those weekdays would be filled with very long walks, and just waiting for Zac to return from work.

I tried to stay busy, trying to work out who this new person was, without Triangl, and without my children. In spite of my lack of financial security, which admittedly I often refused to acknowledge, I acquired a set of porcelain veneers, which was a far more painful and lengthy process than I was expecting. I'd ruined the enamel on my teeth years prior thanks to my eating disorder, and was reasonably self-conscious about my stained teeth. I used injectables regularly, transforming my face into someone completely different, partly out of boredom but mainly I wanted to feel different, to turn myself into someone new. I wanted to shed the feelings I was having: the loss of identity, of passion, of purpose, of meaning in my life, and I hoped by changing how I looked, I'd be able to change how I felt, in some small way at least.

All of these things I was doing were things I'd dreamed of doing while I was 'trapped' with Triangl and Craig, and surprise surprise, they didn't bring me any comfort at all.

Yet, I was just quite desperate to hang on to my identity with Triangl, which was an identity I didn't even like, but it felt better than the reality of being where I was – in Melbourne, without my children and without purpose, which felt like the ultimate fall from grace.

~

In mid 2019, Craig returned to Australia with the boys, but to Sydney, which was where he wanted to live, for it was a better lifestyle than Melbourne in his eyes, and I just wanted my boys back in the same country as me. And so I moved there and rented a house in the same street, to spend half my time there with the boys, and half my time in Melbourne with Zac.

Having the boys with me again felt better, but there was still so much unknown around my financial settlement, and custody too.

Despite all this chaos in my life, the one constant was always Zac. He supported me in whatever stage I was in, and loved me through all of the uncertainty around and within me. We were so madly in love, and it was so comforting to know I had him. The way the world worked, in bringing Zac to me, is something I am still grateful and thankful for every single day. In October 2019, we fell pregnant, which felt like the first big step forward for my new life.

However, with Zac's car-wash business growing and based in Melbourne, it became quickly apparent that my split life between Sydney and Melbourne wasn't going to be sustainable, and while Zac had been unbelievably supportive of my issues and happenings having dominance in our lives, I knew the Sydney situation had to end, and I had to actively push to return to Melbourne, and have Oscar and Oly come with me.

Again, Craig and I found ourselves in a completely awful and messy situation, in which he was only going to leave Monaco and live in Australia if it was Sydney, and I didn't want to be based there anymore. Craig had absolutely zero interest in being in Melbourne despite living there for most of his adult life. It was a backwards step for him which he couldn't get over, and he much preferred the weather and lifestyle in Sydney. On top of this, we were trying to formalise a new financial settlement, which added a monumental amount of stress to everyone's situation.

Craig and I were at war with each other, but also both adamant we didn't want this to affect our children. It's something I am so proud of both of us for doing – always trying to put our children first through all of our issues.

For me, I still held hope we would get through this and come out the other side amicably. I wanted everyone to get along. I'd seen families destroyed by separation, and we not only had a personal separation but a multi-million dollar business separation to handle as well, and we needed to keep those two things apart as much as possible.

Craig eventually returned to Monaco at the start of 2020, and Zac and I had the boys full-time. It still wasn't an ideal situation for our sons, and Craig's absence from the boys' lives was extremely tough on him and them, compounded by the fact the entire world went into lockdown a few months into the year. It was a chaotic and confusing time for everyone, let alone our family who were trying to juggle several major issues, now one of them being we didn't know when the boys would next be able to see their father.

This was particularly stressful for me, being on the receiving end of Craig's frustration when he was understandably upset. It kept me feeling anxious at all times, not knowing when the phone would ring and I'd be subject to a spray over the decisions I'd made. I understood Craig's hurt and his anger – I really did. He had the awful reality of being separated from his children, and as he saw it, and as it accurately had played out, it was because I'd chosen to break up the family.

We were in a severe lockdown in Melbourne, and I was heavily pregnant, so while it was a scary and anxiety-inducing time, there were moments of joy and happiness. Zac and I rented a small house just before the baby's arrival. It was modest, but newly renovated and very well appointed, with four bedrooms. The night before we moved, Zac proposed – a completely unexpected proposal, even though we'd both made it very clear we wanted to spend our lives together. I came home to a dark apartment, and found him on the balcony, in a white suit, on one knee, with a ring. I'd been engaged before but, in my eyes, this may as well have been my first because

I was SO excited to be engaged to this amazing man, and to realize I was going to be with him forever. A few weeks later, our little girl, Beatrice, arrived. My first birth experience with someone by my side, and my god did I need it. I was induced because of the Covid pandemic, largely due to my fear of not being able to have Zac with me as they were imposing restrictions on support partners in the birthing suites and wanted to ensure I could have him there. My labour came on fast, and the midwife didn't believe it was labour until it was too late to have an epidural and I delivered Beatrice without any pain medication. Having Zac by my side was absolutely crucial and I was so thankful to experience it with him.

I was getting used to this new life, one that reminded me more of my pre-Triangl life, and one that made me feel happier than I had in years. It also helped that Beatrice was a dream baby, sleeping like an angel from day one.

I had no choice but to let go of my old self, who was so attached to Triangl, so attached to the high life, and embrace this beautiful family I had in front of me. It was simple, and really healing.

Due to being in lockdown for the majority of that year, my old high-school friends and I started a Facebook group chat, and became really close again, sharing silly stories and frustrated rants over being stuck in our homes. But it felt normal, it felt like real life, and it actually felt really good.

Beatrice brought our family together in such a harmonious way, because she was the first real blood bond of our family, being related to Zac, myself, and Oscar and Oly. It felt so good to have a full little house that felt like a home.

~

I unexpectedly became pregnant again in 2021, finding out in March that year.

We were again thrown into a lockdown, which was to last for most of this year too.

It was around this time that, after numerous failed attempts to settle our financial issues, I sought the advice of a solicitor in Australia to run a process to try and secure my settlement from Triangl. It was a decision I felt was necessary to make. It was less about the money at this point, because I'd seen how I'd been able to live fairly happily with a modest life in Melbourne, but more so because I just wanted it to be over. I wanted Craig and me to stop having this hang over our heads forever; we were three years on from the original settlement and it had been more than enough time for us to settle and move on, after the initial settlement fell over due to issues with payment terms and deadlines, combined with custody challenges regarding the boys.

Craig and I always had a way of going to the trenches and out again fairly quickly and easily, and this was no different. One day we'd be in an awful situation, I'd be in tears and struggling with the enormity of it all, and the next day we'd be chatting light-heartedly about some current event.

At the end of October that year, I had my fourth baby. A little boy, Bobby. An easy pregnancy, as was very fortunately the case with all my babies. His birth was not entirely dissimilar to Beatrice's. I was induced and this time had zero pain thanks to an epidural being administered very early on in the labour process.

By this time, after two years of a lockdown and coming up to four years of issues with Craig after exiting, I was nothing if not exhausted, and I struggled in my post-partum period.

Bobby was not a very easy baby at all. He had a lot of digestive issues, causing him to sleep very little. I found this extremely challenging, and felt it almost unfair to have a fourth be such a hard baby. With sleepless nights being my new normal, and after spending a lot of time at home thanks to a lengthy pandemic, our sweet little house started to feel a bit too small. Bobby didn't have a bedroom and was sleeping in the master wardrobe/bathroom.

It was becoming increasingly frustrating to feel there was no resolution with Craig yet, meaning no clarity over the financial amount I would receive. A lot of my frustrations were also due to fears over the fact I hadn't worked since I exited Triangl, and I was a bit worried as to my own future career prospects as well. I loved having a big family, and being a mother of four, but I was starting to feel somethingI hadn't felt in a long time: ambition. I felt like the old me, the ambitious, business-like side of me was starting to reawaken, and it felt very, very good.

In March 2022, Craig and I settled, finally. An agreement we both felt was fair and a decision we came to together, with the intention of being able to move forward as co-parents amicably.

I was attending a black-tie wedding on the day of signing papers to formalise the settlement, and in between the ceremony and the reception, visited my solicitor's office in central Melbourne, signing for my financial security while dressed in a formal gown.

As much as I know my life had continued to move forward after exiting Triangl (two babies and a fiancé to show for it!), it was after this agreement had been finalised that life truly opened up for me again.

I bought a house in April 2022, in Melbourne, the same suburb where Zac and I met and fell in love, and we moved in a few months later. A beautiful, large, Victorian family home we are currently rebuilding and renovating, and we have all been enjoying having a bit more room for the six of us.

Craig is still in Monaco, and after years of battling through the mud, I consider him a great friend and someone I will always lean on for advice if I need to be told the harsh truth! I have no doubt in my mind we were supposed to be together for a part of our lives. Our connection was, and still is, undoubtedly strong, and as much as I spent many years of my life resenting and pushing Craig away, I'll love him forever for what we did together. Starting Triangl, having our two beautiful sons, navigating a whole new world together, was incredibly special.

The boys have begun seeing Craig regularly again, after the pandemic caused an almighty disruption to being able to access their dad as often as they should have. Admittedly I was hesitant for them to ever leave their Australian home prior to Craig and me settling, whereas now I see the potential for them to get to know their other home, their other life, and it thrills me to know they will experience such special times in a different and very cosmopolitan culture as they grow up.

In November 2022 I launched my own self-named business, offering mentoring and advisory work to founders and start-ups in consumer-led industries. I am so honoured that I am able to support founders and anyone who works in a business who wants to understand how to truly strike a balance between working hard on your career and working hard on yourself. I am deeply passionate about supporting and guiding people on their business journey so that they don't feel they have to choose between having big ambitions and living an emotionally-balanced life. I don't want anyone to achieve the commercial success I did without really feeling good about it.

I launched a podcast in 2023, The Work, with the aim to group mentor as many people as possible on this platform. Finding my voice and my purpose felt so far away from me for many years prior to this, and so now, being able to use my voice in a public way, to support others and help them on their own way in figuring themselves out is a monumental feeling for me.

My long-term goal is to teach younger children how to take care of themselves, mentally, physically and emotionally. We are told so young that we need to pick our career, and to know who we are going to be in the future, when we should instead be given all the emotional, environmental and mental tools to know who we are really, truly are first. I am actively working towards this goal today and will continue to make waves because it is so bloody important to support these children to the full extent we should be.

Zac and I finally started planning our wedding, and were married in June 2023 in Melbourne, with one hundred of our closest family and friends. To have such a supportive man by my side, who encourages me daily to spread my wings, is something I say an internal thank you for almost every single day.

I've never felt happier in my body, both physically and mentally. I feel calm and content, but I'm an ambitious person; I always have been and I always will be, and I'm ready to embark on this new chapter in my life. I truly feel like the best is yet to come.

I've already lived a wild life in the last thirty-nine years, and I'm nowhere near done yet.

In fact, I'm just getting started.

Acknowledgements

Iwould be nothing if not for the people who have believed in me, loved me, inspired me and supported me.

I wrote this book myself, but with much support and guidance along the way.

These are my words of thanks and gratitude to each of you. Thank you to:

Maria – for finding me and getting me back on my business feet after many years away from the business word.

Madd – for so graciously guiding me through the initial book-writing process.

Kelly – for taking a chance on me and allowing me to write how I wanted to.

Craig – for being such a monumental part of my story and for always inspiring me creatively.

Mum and Dad – for giving me a beautiful, safe childhood, and for loving me always.

Janelle – for introducing me to kinesiology, allowing me the space to grow and guiding me to my best version of myself. Sparkly friends forever!

Oscar, Oly, Beatrice and Bobby – the happiness I feel on a daily basis being your mum is like nothing else I ever feel. My life is perfect every day because I have you all in it.

Zac – you are the love of my life. I love how you support and love me just as I am, but even more I love how you encourage me to be better and tell me the tough things only you can get away with telling me. I say a thank you to the universe most nights for you, and I will never not be thankful for the love we have.

And to everyone else who has made me smile, sent me love and lifted me up in some way – I love you. Thank you.